THE SHANGHAI MASSACRE

CHINA'S WHITE TERROR, 1927

PHIL CARRADICE

yd o'r stoc

wn

Pen & Sword

MILITARY

Chen Bo'er: actress, novelist and revolutionist.

First published in Great Britain in 2018 by
PEN AND SWORD MILITARY
an imprint of
Pen and Sword Books Ltd
47 Church Street
Barnsley
South Yorkshire S70 2AS

ISBN 978 1 526738 89 9

Typeset by Aura Technology and Software Services, India
Maps by George Anderson
Printed and bound by CPI Group (UK) Ltd, Croydon, CR0 4YY

Pen & Sword Books Ltd incorporates the imprints of Pen & Sword
Archaeology, Atlas, Aviation, Battleground, Discovery, Family History, History, Maritime, Military, Naval,
Politics, Railways, Select, Social History, Transport, True Crime, Claymore Press, Frontline Books, Leo
Cooper, Praetorian Press, Remember When, Seaforth Publishing and Wharncliffe.

For a complete list of Pen and Sword titles please contact
Pen and Sword Books Limited
47 Church Street, Barnsley, South Yorkshire, S70 2AS, England
email: enquiries@pen-and-sword.co.uk
website: www.pen-and-sword.co.uk

CONTENTS

GLOSSARY

This short glossary covers people, places and organizations that are important when reading the text. There are many others –but these are the significant ones. Use it as a check list, an aide memoir, something to refer back to as the narrative unfolds.

Abbreviations

CPC	Communist Party of China
KMT	Kuomintang, the Nationalist Party formed by Sun Yat-sen
NRA	National Revolutionary Army
PRC	People's Republic of China
ROC	Republic of China (based on Taiwan)

People

General Bai Chongxi	Hewer of Communist Heads
Chiang Kai-shek	Commandant of the NRA and future President of the ROC
Du Yue-sheng	'Big-Eared Du', gangster and ally of Chiang
Emperor Puyi	last of the Manchu Qing emperors
Mao Zedong	future Chairman Mao and Chairman of the PRC
Mikhail Borodin	Soviet adviser to the CPC
Sun Yat-sen	diplomat, philosopher and the father of the nation
Wang Jingwei	Chiang's bitter rival for power
Zhou Enlai	future President of the People's Republic of China

Places of note

Beijing	old imperial capital *aka* Peking
Canton	treaty port/ area in the south
Guangdong	province in the south, China's link with the western world
Hong Kong	treaty port/ area in the south
Nanking	scene of the Nanking Incident of 1927
Shanghai	the beating heart of China
Wuha	western objective of Wang Jingwei

INTRODUCTION

Gather together any disparate group of people; take them from the pub or golf club, from the street or cinema auditorium, and ask them what they know about the Shanghai Massacre of 1927. In 90 percent of the cases, perhaps even more, the response will be blank faces and vacant stares. "Shanghai what, Shanghai when?" they will say. These days the massacre is a largely unknown, almost forgotten incident in history. It is easy to see why.

We have always needed villains in our lives—real ones like Genghis Khan, Napoleon, Kaiser Wilhelm and Adolf Hitler. Fictional characters like Dracula, Bill Sykes or Jaws. Without them our own lives seem puny and unfulfilled; villains are what make the world go around.

In the 1950s and 1960s there existed a thriving media-induced paranoia about the power and influence of one particular group of villains—or good baddies as we children used to call them. Mao Zedong, Chairman Mao as he was universally known: he and his warriors from the People's Republic of China became the new bogeymen of world politics.

Mao's Communist hordes, it was threatened, would soon engulf all of western democracy. Drop the bomb, Mao said—or we were told he said—we don't care. There'll still be enough of us left to pick up the pieces afterwards. Even for the most relaxed and objective of thinkers, people who would otherwise shrug their shoulders and turn back to their radio, book or newspaper that was something of an uncomfortable image.

Such dreadful warnings and dire prophesies suited the rabid anti-Communist ideals of postwar America. They fitted beautifully with the fears engendered by events like the growth of the Cold War, the building of the Berlin Wall, Chinese involvement in the Korean War and, perhaps worst of all, the McCarthy witchhunts back home in America.

Of course, with America happily ensconced as the new global leader and proponent of all things 'good', people believed what the US wanted them to believe. America was at the pinnacle of a new world, gleefully paddling its canoe against the stream and selling off all its many standards and ideals. It was inevitable that American attitudes quickly pervaded all of western culture.

It was cleverly done although, in many cases, not always so subtly achieved as the Americans might have liked. In children's comics, in newspapers, in films, in television

programmes, the message was exported to the world with all the force of a sledgeham-
mer: Communism was a force for evil, an ideology that was preventing self-expres-
sion and, perhaps more importantly, was equally as hell bent on stopping honest men
and women from making an honest buck. Subtle, clever or not, the world lapped it up.

The same media frenzy somehow managed to firmly engulf Mao's Nationalist
opponent Chiang Kai-shek, albeit from a different end of the spectrum. If Mao had
become the bad guy, Chiang was suddenly imbued with the role of prospective
martyr or victim. Mao bad, Chiang good. In the eyes of the west Chiang was quickly
established as a noble freedom fighter, waging a hopeless battle against the onrushing
power of the left-wing thinkers and politicians of the world: "To the world Chiang's
lean, trim, erect figure bespoke resoluteness and determination. His asceticism
and personal austerity seemed to befit a man of dedication to the ideal of a China
resurgent against insuperable odds."*

The fear was that Chiang might always lose the battle. He was already on the back
foot and if he lost, America would lose and, consequently, so would the world. That
fear—and the somewhat skewed understanding of the two sides then fighting for
control of China—has somehow never quite left us.

The end of the Chinese Civil War in 1950 had seen the military defeat and withdrawal
of Chiang Kai-shek and his Nationalists to the island fortress of Taiwan some 110 miles
off the eastern seaboard of China. Chiang was battered but unbowed and on Taiwan,
not unlike the part-time soldiers of Britain's 'Dad's Army' in 1940, Chiang and his force
of two million Nationalists hurled defiance and rhetoric at their conquerors.

All the while they were waiting for the Communist regime back on the mainland to
implode or for the US to fund, organize and take part in a full-scale invasion. It was the
stuff of fairy stories—gallant little Chiang defying Mao Zedong and willing to die for his
beliefs. There may well be an element of truth in that idea but it hides a deeper reality, one
that is more vicious and more violent than the anti-Communist lobby would ever wish to
be made widely known. It begins not just with the Shanghai Massacre but, arguably, with
events that took place long before that seminal moment in Chinese—and world—history.

The story of the Chinese revolution that ended thousands of years of imperial rule
is complex, compelling and confusing, something that is not helped by the unusual
nature and remoteness of the country and by the names of people and places that
are nothing if not alien to western eyes and ears. Reading about the history of China
is a bit like reading *War and Peace*. You are constantly forgetting which character is
which and having to refer back to the 'cast list'.

If this book does nothing else it will attempt to provide a measure of clarity to a very
unclear and confusing time. It will, hopefully, intrigue the reader and make places,

---

* Chiang's obituary *The New York Times*, 6 April 1975

Maj Gen Smedley Butler arrives to inspect the US Marine barracks in Shanghai, 1927. (USMC)

people and the problems that they faced come alive on the page. It is historically correct but the text is intended to be accessible and to read almost like a novel. It is meant to hold the reader to the end, helping him or her understand the problems of China in the modern world.

The demise of wicked imperialism in China, together with the creation of a pure Nationalist regime and the creeping virus of Communist ideals, might well be a simplistic version of events. But it is a process that is fascinating and one that does not stop in 1912 with the abdication of the last emperor.

Like all revolutions, the ending of the Qing dynasty was not clear cut or final—the end of despotism, the arrival of democracy. The struggles and the fighting went on, for many years. It was a period marked by dispute, by warfare and by murder, with thousands being killed and the countryside marked for ever by the depredations of change and, to coin a good old fashioned cliché, by man's inhumanity to man.

On a wider plain, some understanding of what went on and a little knowledge about the chaotic nature of social and political unrest that preceded and followed the massacre at Shanghai—the beating heart of China as someone once called the city—is essential if anyone is ever going to understand the history of the 20th century.

Dutch marines arriving in Shanghai, 1927.

China might be distant and remote for most of us but it has played a pivotal role in the demise of capitalist regimes and the steady growth of left-wing ideas and beliefs during the last hundred years. Along with the USSR and the US, China became one of the key elements of the 20th-century world. It will undoubtedly continue to play a vital role in the decades ahead.

And that, of course, brings us once more to the Shanghai Massacre and to the White Terror that followed it—the massacre being the events of 12 April 1927, the White Terror covering the months of murder and mayhem that followed. They are events that show Chiang Kai-shek not as a gallant freedom fighter but as a self-interested, brutal and violent warlord. Or was he? Arguably, that view is as one-sided and as far from the truth as the American-induced panic of the 1950s. At the end of the day we can, each of us, only define his actions as we see fit. As Olivette Otele has said, in our understanding of people and places: "We have created grey areas that allow us to ignore sinister sides of human nature. 'Man is a wolf to man', as the old Latin proverb has it; a magnificent beast capable of bending his or her own rules and ruthlessly redefining morals to reach his or her goals."

The Shanghai Massacre marks the beginning of the Chinese Civil War. On and off, with moments of cooperation like the coming together of Chiang and Mao to fight off the clutches of the Japanese Empire during the Second World War, that conflict

The 3rd Plenary Session of the 2nd Central Committee of the Kuomintang of China (March 1927). Front row (R to L): Wu Yuzhang, Jing Hengyi, Chen Youren, Song Ziwen, Song Qingling, Sun Ke, Tan Yankai, Xu Qian, Gu Mengyu, Ding Weifen; Second row (R to L): Zhu Jiqing, Lin Boqu, Mao Zedong, Peng Zemin, Yu Shude, Chen Qiyuan, Chen Maoxiu, Ding Chaowu, Dong Biwu, Jiang Hao; Third row (R to L): Xie Jin, Xu Suhun, Deng Yanda, Yun Daiying, Chen Gongbo, Zhan Dabei, Xia Xi, Wang Faqin, Wang Leping, Zhou Qigang.

lasted until 1950. Finally, it resulted in a Communist victory and the establishment of the Chinese People's Republic.

Had Chiang triumphed in the civil war, Mao and the Communists would undoubtedly have taken up a similar stance, adopted a similar posture to their defeated enemy—if they had been allowed to live. Fate declared otherwise.

History might well belong to the victors but that does not always mean that they will be granted a whitewashed or sanitized reputation. Sometimes the very opposite is true, which is exactly what happened in China. In order to achieve that, however, events like the Shanghai Massacre had to be covered up or hidden. How else could Chiang Kai-shek be placed into the role of saintly would-be martyr? Perhaps it is time to set the record straight.

1. THE WHITE TERROR BEGINS

It is four o'clock in the morning of 12 April 1927 and the Chinese city of Shanghai is still largely asleep. In those dim but expectant moments on the rim of a new day everything pauses, everything sits still and waiting.

The last seconds of cloaking darkness cast a silence that lies thickly over people and places. It is the same in all countries, in all nations and in all parts of the world. However, here, in China, in cities like Shanghai, it is the contrast that is most obvious—the contrast between that sudden silence and the incessant murmuring of the night. It is as if the lives of the people, lives normally lived on the edge, have suddenly come to a halt.

On the riverfront the sampans, ferries and skiffs lie solidly and silently against their wharfs. The Yangtze Delta still pushes wavelets against the vessels and the jetties but somehow they make no noise. The boats that normally rock in the swell now sit defiantly still in the water. The usual slap of wood on wall, a sound found in

Shanghai, bustling port and commercial centre.

A Kuomintang parade in Gannan.

any port or boatyard on the river, seems to have disappeared even though the boats are open to the elements and the tide.

Below the decks of the larger vessels the crews are draped, motionless across the decks. Even their snores are muted and the normally incessant patter of rodents' feet across the scuppers and in the bilges is finally still and silent.

Across the port and out into the sprawling city streets tired rickshaw drivers lie curled like giant ammonites in the backs of their vehicles. The lucky ones, the richer ones who can afford such luxuries, are covered by blankets that have, all day, doubled as padding for the customer's seats.

In the opium dens nothing moves. The lights are out and late smokers, drugged into heavenly oblivion, lie comatose and unthinking. Only the sickly sweet smell of the dope betrays the function of the shops. Dogs and cats that have prowled restlessly throughout the nighttime hours have now, at last, taken to their beds, their places of sanctuary where they will rest and fall instantly asleep; children turn on their futons and dream of pirate junks and sampans that will one day carry them across the bounding East China Sea; men and women snore and slumber on, dreaming of wealth that will probably never come. For a few brief moments there is peace in the city.

And then a sudden bugle call splits the predawn air, cutting like a razor through the darkness. It is strident, startling the birds that are still roosting in the spidering bushes of Shanghai's parks. It shakes the stunted branches of the camphor trees

Opium-smoking, 1906. (Sanshichiro Yamamoto)

along the city's streets and alleyways. The bugle call alarms the birds, causing them to rise like giant mosquito clouds into the air. They squawk and cry and whirl away to safer, less noisy locations.

With the last notes of the bugle finally echoing into nothingness, the dogs that have so recently settled to sleep begin to shift once more. Slowly, stretching their lean bodies into wakefulness, they begin to turn and rise to their feet. These last bugle notes are on that deep-rooted wavelength that only dogs can ever know and soon, fur rising like icicles along their spines, the howl of the wakened animals is echoing from the back streets and gardens. In unison they bounce off the thin wooden walls of the city's shacks and houses.

The noise of the blaring bugle and the shrieking of the wakened animals disturb people in many different parts of the city. From the International Settlement and the French Concession to the dwellings of the rich Chinese merchants and bankers they set off a thin but compelling frisson of fear. Principally, however, it is in the poorer quarters where the workers live and try their best to survive, that the bugle call is noted most.

For those who have an acute or more than normal awareness of the tensions that have recently fallen across the city it is a call to arms. These few individuals have some understanding of the lurking dangers of the time, an understanding of the potential for disaster that this bugle call holds. It is a warning to be heeded—and heeded quickly.

An execution takes place in the street.

With a sudden lurch of their bellies the more astute listeners are instantly awake, tracing the bugle call to the headquarters of General Chiang Kai-shek, commander of the National Revolutionary Army and the most powerful man in the region. Most of them have never seen Chiang; some have caught a brief glimpse as he drives past in his car. They all know of him, however, and Chiang gives every single one of them a good reason to be afraid.

For others, less aware or perhaps wrapped more deeply in the cocoon of sleep, the noise is no more than a distant growling at the corner of their dreams. For them the last few moments of innocence will continue to be blissful.

The choice is simple: turn over and go back to sleep or dress quickly and flee. Hundreds choose the former option. It is a fateful decision, in some cases a fatal one. It is a decision that condemns far too many of the half-wake workers to an unforgiving end. Within minutes of the warning bugle, bands of thugs, operating under the auspices of the China Mutual Advancement Society, descend on the houses of the sleeping victims. They are looking for union men, for Communists and for any left-wing supporters they can find. They are looking, in fact, for opponents of General Chiang Kai-shek.

Whirling through the streets like the typhoons and whirlwinds that the area knows only too well, the thugs smash open the flimsy doors or crash through windows that are locked but provide little security. Some of the more evil-natured simply stand waiting, menacing and perhaps more terrifying for that, in the darkness. In a

General Chiang Kai-shek in martial pose.

drumming tattoo of anger and fury some of them slam their swords and staves against the ground or fence posts demanding that the men inside the houses come out to meet their fate.

Most of the attackers from this first wave of assaults are members of the criminal triads that proliferate in Shanghai. In particular they come from the Green Gang, one of the most vicious and effective of all the city's underworld groups. They are deeply embroiled in crime: it is commonly said that there is almost no criminal activity in the city that does not admit to the hands of the Green Gang some-where in the mess.

Big-Eared Du, gangster leader.

Chiang has patronized the Green Gang and cleverly enrolled them on his side. He has bribed their leader Du Yue-sheng and other headmen, people like the policeman-cum-rob-ber-cum-jewel thief Huang Jinrong, with promises of money and power. He has judged them well, these bastions of criminal society; the bandit leaders fall in happily at his side.

For the ordinary members of the gangs the prospect of violence is more than enough. For them the wielding of power starts and ends with the brutality of the riot and the mêlée. The taking of life—or the losing of it—warrants little more than a wry, inscru-table smile or shrug. At the most basic level, they like violence. Nevertheless, the gang members have a pragmatic view of life. None of the Green Gang will, today, pass up on the chance of robbery or looting from the houses of their victims, particularly if they gain access to any of the foreign legations.

For their task this morning Green Gang members have dressed in the traditional blue dungarees worn by workers all over the country. They also sport white armbands—that bear the words '*Kung*' or Workers—startlingly bright against the blue denim of the dungarees. All are armed, usually with knives and clubs, but some carry swords and pistols.

For those union men and Communists who are caught in their houses or as they emerge yawning and disorientated from their doorways, there are beatings and, even at this early stage, many are killed before they know what is happening. Those who manage to escape the initial onslaught are pursued in a terrifying frenzy as they flee or try to make a stand.

As dawn breaks above Shanghai dozens of the victims are corralled into groups and then executed on the city streets. Beheading is the preferred method of execution although at this early stage of the massacre many are shot or simply clubbed to death.

Chiang Kai-shek on the cover
of *Time* magazine's April 1927
edition.

In that strange, disconcerting acceptance that seems to signify the Chinese character, once they are lined up and made to kneel before their executioners, many of the Communists bow their heads to the executioners. Bowing to the inevitable as scholars would have it. But that would be too simple a description, too simple by far—and yet still they kneel there in the streets and wait. It is, perhaps, an acceptance that this is their fate, that this is how it has always been intended to finish.

District offices of the trade unions are also targeted. Here members of the Green Gang have little chance of dishing out beatings, arrests and executions, at least not at this time of the morning. Party officials and staff will not be here until eight or nine o'clock but there is still the prospect of looting and the thought of wanton destruction is always a welcome possibility. The triads go happily about their work. In some instances the Communists try to fight back but such opposition is rare. They are outnumbered and, as far as violence is concerned, totally outclassed by the gangs.

Inevitably, looting—mostly but not totally the preserve of the Green Gang—continues for some time. Accusations made later that Chiang's men have confiscated money and possessions from their victims are met with blank denials. So too is the belief that 'donations' have been extorted from wealthy Shanghai businessmen. Maybe, maybe not, but either way it is hard to believe that the executioners are altruistic enough not to have helped themselves to a little something on the side.

It is not long before Chiang sends in his soldiers to assist the triad gangs. Death and destruction need to be more organized, more controlled, he feels. The gangs have done their work—the initial assault was both brutal and terrifying—but now it needs more than a simple blunt-headed machine like the triads. Now it needs a more formal approach to death.

More arrests and more beheadings quickly follow in the wake of the soldiers as blood, quite literally, flows down the city streets. Not for nothing does *Time* magazine later bestow the epithet of 'Hewer of Communist Heads' on Chiang's accomplice and supporter General Bai Chongxi. Bai is the man with direct responsibility for the massacre and for the killings that will follow over the next few weeks. The White Terror has now truly begun.

It is not all mute acceptance and bowing to the inevitable from the Communists and trade unionists, however. In Nantao and Chapei, two industrial sections of Shanghai, there is heavy fighting as workers' pickets, militia units formed in readiness for just such an event as this, put up stern resistance. The battles last until ten in the morning when the final pickets are either shot or disarmed by soldiers of the NRA and by

Shanghai, the Old City, as seen today, little changed in ninety years. (w:User:PHG)

A contemporary cartoon showing the massacre taking place.

units of the China Mutual Advancement Society. According to Chiang's compatriot and fellow army commander Pai Ch'ung-hsi over 300 Communists are arrested and more than two thousand rifles seized.

The intervention of the soldiers destroys, for once and for all, any illusion that Chiang Kai-shek is neutral or not involved in the killings. It is not a matter that concerns the hunted Communists: they are simply trying to survive. But for the foreigners in the legations it is an important message and consideration.

While death was left in the hands of the Green Gang there was always the option of shielding behind anonymity but not now. These are Chiang's soldiers on the streets and they are operating on his orders. Not that he has ever wanted to hide the fact. It is just that now the director and the direction of the assaults are clear to everyone, Chinese and foreign 'barbarians' alike. His hand is the guiding force behind the massacre.

There are reports, albeit unsubstantiated, of Communist victims being thrown alive into the furnaces of railway locomotives on this dreadful day of death and destruction. There is no evidence for such behaviour but, given the hatred and the blood lust that undoubtedly envelopes Chiang's forces on this fatal morning, such actions could well have taken place.

The Rise and Fall of the Green Gang

The origins of the infamous Green Gang are complex. This criminal organization had its roots in a perfectly respectable Buddhist sect or society known as the Luojiaco but by the middle years of the 18th century it had become considerably more secular than was first intended.

The society was important for the workers on China's Grand Canal, the route used to transport grain to the market place. It gave invaluable social support to these boatmen, providing services for things like funerals and accommodation for men on their journeys.

The activities of the society were frowned on by the authorities and their growing importance in the minds of workers soon became perceived as a threat by the authoritarian Chinese government. In 1768 the emperor ordered the destruction of their temples and the society was proscribed. All that this achieved was to drive them underground.

By now the society was known as Friends of the Way of Tranquillity and Purity but, already, its members were hovering on the fringes of crime. Shanghai, where the society based itself, was an ideal centre for criminal activity, particularly when the port was opened up as a gateway to foreign trade. A disjointed legal environment in the city gave criminals a loophole and with a high level of internal immigration Shanghai offered many opportunities to make money. The society became heavily involved in the opium trade.

With so many Chinese flocking to the city, organizations such as the Green Gang—as it now became—were based on family connections and home turf, not unlike the Mafia in America. The 'secret' element of the gang was established.

By the start of the 20th century the Green Gang was in control of almost all criminal activity in Shanghai and had become totally corrupt. And that was how things stayed until the defeat of Chiang Kai-shek in 1949. With the coming of the Communists the leaders of the Green Gang decided it was time to move and the gang relocated its heroin refineries to Hong Kong.

Their time in Hong Kong was not easy as the Green Gang soon became involved in bitter rivalries and feuds with local drug gangs and heroin syndicates. They were outnumbered and outclassed and by the 1960s the Green Gang was dead.

At the very least the rumour of men being burned alive is greeted with shouts of joy and woops of delight from the Green Gang members. Rumour or fact, the story has been remembered and perpetuated both in legend and literature: "'[They] don't shoot, they throw them alive into the boiler of the locomotive,' he was saying. 'And now they're whistling ...' The sentry was approaching again. Silence, except for the pain ... The soldiers were coming to fetch two prisoners in the crowd who could not get up. No doubt being burned alive entitled one to special, though limited, honours: transported on a single stretcher, almost on top of each other.'"*

A blanket of terror has now fallen like a dark winter night across the city of Shanghai. It is so palpable, so tangible that you can almost reach out and touch it. Even those who are not involved in trade union activity are gathered into its pall. It is an understandable emotion.

People are terrified by the killings, by the strutting Green Gang thugs and by the sight of decapitated bodies in the streets. They are frightened that they will be next and anyone who has ever had connections with the Communist Party of China (CPC) will quickly seek to distance themselves from the organization. It is no accident that over the coming weeks and months membership of the CPC will drop from over 58,000 to a miniscule 10,000.

Chiang Kai-shek will later write in his diary that his "heart was lifted" by the knowledge that Communists were being dealt with all over the city. No single group requires killing more than the Communists, he declares, going on to state that he would rather mistakenly kill a thousand innocent people than allow even one Communist to escape. The diary entries are for his personal use but it is still incendiary stuff.

After the initial killings, the culling of Chiang's opponents gathers pace, more or less unhindered. Hundreds of Communists and trade unionists, skilled or lucky enough to have escaped the initial massacre, are hunted down, arrested and taken prisoner. There is no guarantee of safety or survival, however, not even for these captives; the killings will continue.

In some respects those who are hacked down or shot in the opening hours of the terror are the lucky ones. At least for them there is an

General Bai, the 'Hewer of Communist Heads'.

---

* André Malraux, *Man's Fate*

end of fear, an end of suffering. For those arrested there awaits only beatings, torture and execution. There seems to be little rhyme or reason to the selection. The massacre has unleashed a wave of anti-Communist emotion and the Shanghai Massacre or 'the 12 April Incident', as the day of killing is sometimes known, is certainly not an end in itself.

Soon the massacre spreads beyond Shanghai to other cities, even to the villages and the surrounding countryside. At Canton in the south the military forces act with particular violence. Communists—or even those suspected of being Communists—are simply roped together and herded to the local parade ground. There they are summarily shot. No trial, no debate, execution is the clear order of the day.

Some estimates state that well over than 300 people are murdered on 12 April alone with another 1,000 being arrested by Chiang's troops. Their fate will be determined later. Many more have simply disappeared, vanished never to resurface, as private vendettas begin to take effect. And that is just the start. In some reports the death toll on 12 April and in the coming weeks of the White Terror has been set at between five and ten thousand. Within the year the figure will climb to an almost unbelievable 300,000.

For the ordinary people they will never again hear an early morning knock on the door or the rattle of something unknown and unknowable in the darkness of the night without a sudden thumping of the heart and a huge lurch of the belly. That is their legacy from the 12 April massacre.

British troops guard the legation.

Zhou Enlai, 1927.

The highest profile victim of the Massacre and the White Terror is the writer, philosopher and librarian Li Dazhao. He is not present in Shanghai on 12 April. But Li, a founder of the CPC along with his friend and comrade Chen Duxiu, is arrested while sheltering in the Russian embassy in Beijing. The embassy is stormed by Nationalist forces—there is no sanctuary anywhere and the foreign legations and embassies are as vulnerable to Chiang's Nationalists as the humblest of workers' houses. Li is hanged, along with nineteen others, on 28 April.

Chiang Kai-shek is well satisfied with his work. Determined to break the power of the Communists once and for all, on the surface at least he seems to have succeeded.

Among the prisoners taken is Zhou Enlai, the future premier of Communist China and at that time commander of the workers' military units in Shanghai. He is lucky. In the days prior to the massacre there had been a plot to assassinate him, part of a complex plan intended to tie in with the actions of 12 April. Unfortunately for Chiang and the Nationalists—but more than lucky for Zhou—the plan fails, dismally.

Zhou Enlai and his comrade in arms Wang Shouhua, head of the General Labour Committee of the CPC, are both earmarked for death in the hours before the mass killings are due to begin. Their deaths will be a warning and a 'frightener' for the Communists in the city.

Wang is beaten up, pinioned and then strangled on the eve of the massacre, 11 April, when he arrives for dinner at the house of gangster Du Yue-sheng. Chiang has given his new ally an important role to play, not just as accomplice to the events of 12 April but, as a way of embroiling him deeper into the plot, he is also to be employed as an executioner. The killing of Wang is a brutal, calculated and cold-blooded assassination but it is not as efficiently done as Du would have liked: "Thinking he was dead, the hoodlums stuffed him into a hessian sack and drove to waste ground outside the French concession to bury the body there. As they finished digging the grave they heard Wang moaning, so they interred him alive."*

Buried alive or buried dead, it does not matter to Du but as a professional he would have liked it to have been done with a little more finesse. 'Big-Eared Du' as the gang

---

*   Jonathan Fenby, *Generalissimo: Chiang Kai-shek and the China He Lost*

leader is universally known, is an ambitious man. He is keen to make the move from crime to politics and finding that there is little to choose between the two is happy to fall in with Chiang's plans. Strangling Wang Shouhua is a matter of no consequence to him.

For some reason Zhou Enlai manages to escape the fate of Wang. On 11 April he too is meant to meet his end in the same grizzly fashion. However, he is not killed, merely arrested. Early in the evening he arrives for dinner at the headquarters of Si Lie, commander of the 26th Army and soon finds himself in custody. It is a mistake but it saves his life. Once in custody Zhou is relatively safe—at least until the following day.

As dawn breaks on 12 April Zhou Enlai realizes that while he is now languishing in the hands of the military: his real captor is Chiang Kai-shek and the Nationalists. He fears the worst. For a while his fate hangs in the balance but strangely, before the end of the day, he is suddenly and unexpectedly released from captivity. The reasons for Zhou's release are unclear. He is, perhaps, too high profile a figure to perish in the 12 April Massacre; perhaps it is another mistake. According to some sources Chiang has deliberately allowed him to slip away in order to repay a debt he racked up when Zhou helped him escape the clutches of a rampaging mob several years earlier. Whatever the reason, Zhou is free and he disappears gratefully into the night. Arguably, allowing him to escape the death squads and to enjoy freedom to continue opposing the Nationalists is a dreadful political mistake. Deliberate or not, it is one that Chiang will live to regret.

*

In the wake of the 12 April massacre the Communists and trade unionists try desperately to stage some sort of rearguard action. The old adage that their powder is damp is, to say the least, a terrible understatement.

Most members of the Kuomintang have already given Chiang their blessing, their tacit approval. Even so, he is still immediately denounced by thirty-nine members of the KMT Central Committee, including his mother-in-law, the widow of his previous mentor Sun Yat-sen. Even Chiang's own son, the young Chiang Ching-kuo then studying in Moscow, is unhappy and appalled by what has gone on. He immediately denounces his father as "a traitor and murderer".

The Comintern eagerly seizes on Chiang Ching-kuo's disapproval. It is, after all, good publicity in the face of what appears to be total disaster in Shanghai. The newspaper *Izvestia* happily publishes a letter from the young Chiang—how genuine it actually is remains a matter of conjecture—stating that "I do not know you as my father any more."

At this stage words mean very little, either to Chiang Kai-shek or to the hundreds of dead bodies still lying in the streets of Shanghai. It is all too little, too late and is totally ineffective. Chiang Kai-shek is now determined on his course and will follow his star to the end. He simply shrugs off the comments and the condemnation of his political friends and enemies. His son is a dispensable asset. It is regrettable but there are now bigger issues and more at stake than filial relationships.

Within a few weeks, Chiang defiantly forms a new government in Nanjing. Its intention is to rival the "Communist tolerant" national government that has been recently established in Wuhan and will show no mercy for anyone not fitting in with Chiang's ideals. He is now firmly set on a policy of destroying all Communist influence in China. That includes the previously much-valued support of the Soviet Union.

The Comintern immediately breaks off relations with the KMT, Chiang's Nationalist Party. It is no more than he expected but by this stage Chiang Kai-shek neither worries nor cares. He has received their money and their arms; losing their friendship is, he feels, a price worth paying for dispensing with the treacherous CPC.

There is little else that the Communists can do but, after discussion, some of the braver ones finally decide on action rather than words. Even now they do not propose to fight—which is all that the members of Du's Green Gang really understand. What these thugs cannot come to terms with is the notion that most of the Communists simply want to shout and scream rather than resort to the knife, the club or the gun.

Despite the anxiety that has fallen like a shroud across the city of Shanghai, on 13 April, the day after the massacre, thousands of workers and students gather up enough courage to begin a protest march. They walk in a huge heaving mass to Chiang's headquarters, the home of the 2nd Division, 26th Army. They plan to demonstrate, peacefully, against the previous day's actions of Chiang Kai-shek and his minions. It is a courageous and desperate throw of the dice—and, of course, it is doomed to failure.

The consequences of the march and of the attendant protest could have been predicted. In a scene reminiscent of the slaying of protesters outside the Winter Palace after the Russian defeat by Japan in 1905, soldiers guarding the barracks open fire on the crowd. At least a hundred are killed, many more wounded and maimed.

Another hundred? To Chiang it hardly matters. He has gone too far to stop now and he knows that figure will be doubled, tripled, multiplied by hundreds in the weeks ahead.

He dissolves the Communist Shanghai government and closes down all of the labour unions. A similar fate awaits all organizations that have affiliation of any sort to the Communists. In their place Chiang will create alternative unions.

Eight years on, the Chinese Reds were almost totally exterminated.

Mao Zedong in 1926.

The difference is, of course, that all of the new units will have strong links to his Nationalist party.

Chiang's coup d'état has been sudden and effective but it has not been perfect and the remnants of the CPC, men like Zhou Enlai and Mao Zedong, are still alive and operating. Many Communists go into hiding in cities like Canton and Hong Kong. But there they are quickly hunted down by Chiang's troops. The countryside, in particular those areas where the power of the KMT has not yet reached and the wild lands of the plains, are a far safer bet.

And that is where the real survivors, the ones who will stay alive throughout the White Terror now go. They might be in hiding in the countryside outside Shanghai, keeping a low profile. They might be bloodied and battered. But they are still there and even Chiang knows that it is only a matter of time before they will rise again, stronger and more determined than ever.

However, for the time being at least, there can be little doubt that by his actions on 12 April and over the ensuing weeks Chiang Kai-shek has created a one-party dictatorship in China. To begin with it seems to be enough but there is a long way still to go before Chiang will be able to feel truly safe.

The year 1927 is to be one of continued disruption and chaos. It is a period of upheaval that has rarely been matched in Chinese history. In order to understand it fully—the events before, during and after the Shanghai Massacre—we have to go back and try to come to terms with the nature of the country, its people and the problems of the reformers who attempted to bring China kicking and screaming into the modern world. It is the only way to make sense of what often seems like a convoluted and confusing series of incidents.

2. LOOKING BACK

China is one of the largest countries in the world, covering nearly four million square miles of the earth's surface. Russia and Canada might be larger but they do not have the diversity, either in topography or climate, in people or languages that you will find in China.

Up until the beginning of the 19th century China was even larger than it is today with the Chinese Empire spreading out to include Mongolia and regions to the north. It also took in Taiwan (also known as Formosa) and several other islands off the eastern coast. Large sections of neighbouring territory like Korea, Burma and Indo-China were also under Chinese rule or control.

Even now the country stretches 3,600 miles from north to south with the result that the Chinese people, as they always have been, are subjected to extremes of snow, heat, rain and violent storms on a regular basis. Such an enormous land mass gives extreme diversity of weather. On the same day it might well be snowing in the north where the temperature will be far below freezing, while 3,000 miles to the south people will undoubtedly be sweltering in 100 percent humidity.

More than 700 million of China's vast population are Han people, considered to be the true Chinese. The rest are national minorities such as the Mongolians or Tibetans. In the main the bulk of the population is gathered together in the east of the country, leaving the bleak western steppes sparsely populated and undeveloped. Again, this is just as it has always been.

In the north China is guarded and sealed off from its neighbours by the vast emptiness of the Gobi Desert; in the west it is bordered by the Himalaya, mighty Mount Everest rising to 29,035 feet on the Chinese–Nepalese border. The country's two main rivers, the Yangtze and the Yellow, rise here in the west and sweep down across the plains to exit the land mass on the eastern rim of the country. On their journey to the sea the rivers cross deserts and cut giant gullies through mountains and dense forests. They, and China's other smaller rivers, provide a series of defensive barriers and communication channels across otherwise hostile territory. They also offer irrigation but, even so, little more than 10 percent of the country has ever been properly cultivated.

Industry came late to China, so much so that the Marxist ideologists of the USSR have often claimed that the country can never be truly communist as it has not undergone urban revolution. This has meant that the main thrust of China's economic output has always been rural. Even that has tended to be of a subsistence variety, peasant farmers growing just enough food to live on and only rarely selling excess produce in the open market. The soil has been unproductive, a problem that has often led to flood, famine and hardship for the peasant farmers.

There has never been fair distribution of land and wealth in China. In 1950, when Mao Zedong came to power, as much as 70 percent of the land rested in the hands of just 10 percent of the population. Things began to change under Mao but it has been—and will continue to be—a slow process.

For thousands of years China was an imperial kingdom, ruled by a number of different dynasties and emperors. One of the first of these was Emperor Qinshi Huangdi who created a series of provinces within the country and a bureaucratic central government to oversee the management of his Empire. From the beginning there were problems in even attempting to control such an enormous country from one central base.

As a result of this practice, it was inevitable that there would be times of trouble and dispute. Qinshi and many of his successors regularly found themselves having to deal with the prospect of revolt, invasion, rebellion and usurpers. Dynasties changed on an almost routine basis, often as the result of military activity. The population of China remained vast, meaning that while their rulers might change, for the people of the country life invariably went on as normal.

The final imperial dynasty, the Manchu Qing dynasty, held power from 1644 until its eventual demise in 1912 but with such a diverse and widespread nation it needed an efficient and well-organized administration to rule the country effectively and as one entity. The Qings were neither.

Chinese peasants working in a simple hut.

Marco Polo

Whatever his credibility, Marco Polo remains the most significant figure in the opening up of China to western trade and influence. He was not an adventurer in the mode of Francis Drake or Vasco da Gama but he was a trader and a man who was intensely interested in the foreign territories that he saw on his travels.

Marco Polo was born in Venice in 1254 and picked up the basics of the trading business from his father Niccolo and his uncle Maffeo. They had both travelled widely in Asia and had even met with the great Kublai Khan. The young Marco was enthralled by their tales and when the opportunity came to join them on another tour of the east he grabbed it.

It was to be a journey that lasted twenty-four years, Marco, his father and uncle, travelling by camel along the Silk Road. They arrived in China in the year 1275 where they were welcomed at the court of Kublai Khan. Over the next twenty years Marco traded and worked. According to what he later wrote he became a valued adviser to the emperor and even held the position of governor of Yangzhou for three years. Such claims have, inevitably, been challenged by modern scholars.

The adventures of Marco Polo were written down in his book *The Marvels of the World* and included events like raids by bandits on the caravan that he and his relatives had joined. They eventually left China—somewhat surreptitiously—and arrived back in Venice to find the city at war with Genoa. They had travelled nearly 15,000 miles during their twenty-four-year sojourn in the east.

Because of the war with Genoa, Marco was imprisoned and it was in his jail cell that he dictated his famous account to fellow-writer Rustichello da Pisa. Once again, modern critics have questioned his authorship, However it was written, Marco was released from prison in 1299, married, became a wealthy trader and businessmen and raised three children. He died in January 1324 and was buried in the Church of San Lorenzo in Venice.

Marco Polo's book, sometimes called *The Travels of Marco Polo*, was the first detailed account of China, its people and their interactions with a man from Europe. It inspired Christopher Columbus and was a significant influence on cartography. Perhaps more importantly, his travels and his book mark the beginning of significant western interest in China.

As a result both of ineptitude and the enormity of the task, China became fragmented, various regions or parcels of land coming under the control of warlords and local rulers who were, effectively, masters of everything they surveyed. Like the Norman marcher lords of early medieval England they held sway over territories where "the Emperor's writ truly does not run".

The warlords and the emperor might control the country but somewhere in the region of 80 percent of China's population—maybe even more—have always been peasants or subsistence farmers. They endured a basic, hand-to-mouth existence where scratching a frugal living from the soil was tenuous, to say the least. It was a way of life that brought few benefits and little reward.

Even by the beginning of the 20th century women, in particular, had few rights. They were the property of their fathers or, occasionally, their uncles and unless their 'owner' had access to money to pay a dowry to any prospective partner they were likely to stay single for the rest of their lives. Women were considered a drain on the family and it was not unusual for newborn baby girls to be cast aside and left in the fields to die from exposure.

Qing army officers.

And yet that remains something of a generalization which was not always the full case. Chinese culture has always been advanced, at least for everyone apart from the very poor. For the 10 percent of those who had the time, money and inclination to enjoy it, life in China could be highly profitable—at least from a cultural point of view.

It might be something of a cliché but while the people from the rest of the world were living in caves and fighting each other with bone axes, many of the inhabitants of this amazing country were leading a relatively refined, even delicate existence with standards of living that were incomparable to those in the west several centuries later. In literature and philosophy, in science and in art, the Chinese set standards that Europeans—even if they had the desire and technology to visit the country—would have found beyond their levels of comprehension.

Techniques and crafts such as paper and book production, silk making and enamelling, pottery firing and the use of gunpowder were commonplace in China long before they became familiar to western peoples. The Chinese did not think such things remarkable but those Europeans who encountered them for the first time could hardly contain themselves in their greedy desire to possess such items.

Unfortunately, however, the country was for many years isolated from the rest of the world. It was not just isolated: as a result of being cut off from other cultures the people became inward looking. This was, in many respects, a fatal flaw and a surprising one considering that China was then and still is surrounded or fringed by no fewer than fourteen other countries.

Barricaded in or blocked off from the rest of civilization by the Himalaya, by the Gobi Desert and by mighty oceans that required skill and courage to cross, the Chinese people believed their country to be the centre of the world. In keeping with this belief, they called their homeland Zhongguo—the middle kingdom, a land situated between heaven and earth.

They had nothing to learn, the Chinese people felt, from the barbarians or foreign devils as the few intrepid explorers who managed to reach the country were known. Many of the in-comers, astounded by what they saw, were quickly assimilated into the Chinese culture but little was ever given or taken back by a people who knew that their culture, their way of life, was markedly superior to anything the foreigners could offer.

It was a xenophobic attitude that bordered on the delusional and perpetuated the Chinese view of themselves as being both different and superior. The country, its people and their way of life, undoubtedly held a fascination for many outsiders and as the prospects of trade and cultural links developed it was something that grew in strength.

Adventurers such as Marco Polo, one of the earliest European visitors to China, had paved the way. He had come, hardly expecting to find such a different culture and was often at a loss to describe exactly what he saw. The Chinese, he said, burned black rocks that they had dug out of the ground in order to give them heat, little realizing that he was describing coal, a fossil fuel which would, in the centuries ahead, power the Industrial Revolution and change the entire western world.

By his travels and writings Marco Polo opened the door to Chinese exploration. He was the first but soon improved seamanship and ship design in the 17th century gradually began to open up the mysterious worlds beyond the Himalaya. The Chinese people remained obdurate: let the barbarians come, they are not needed.

Above: Sampans, traditional Chinese craft.

Left: Kublai Khan, painted shortly after his death.

The famous Silk Road—surely a misnomer as there was not one road but many, including a treacherous sea route—was an ancient network of trade roads to and from the west. These routes date from several centuries BC and were well established but never safe or secure. They were routes that connected China to the empires of Rome and Persia—connected them, yes, but always at the behest and control of China. Along this trail were sent silks and spices, jade and saffron, tortoise shells and feathers. It was invariably Chinese silks and other produce, a process of one-way traffic that produced goods and items craved, in particular, by the women of the west. The travellers or traders did bring back some limited western ideas but, more importantly, they carried a great deal of western money into China.

The Silk Road and an Unexpected Gift

The Silk Road, in more recent times. (Fulvio Spada)

The Silk Road—or the Silk Route as it should be more accurately called—was not one but a complete network of trade routes between China and Europe. These were both terrestrial and maritime routes that were founded during the Han dynasty and lasted for hundreds of years until the Ottoman Empire boycotted trade with China in 1453.

In the main it was a well-organized and efficiently run system that provided western countries with a wide variety of goods, ranging from silks and linen to gunpowder, carpets and fine china. It was a reciprocal system with western goods and items—horses in particular—being sent the other way. Inns and hostels, guest houses as they were called, were established along the route, each of them located exactly one day's ride by horse or camel from the next.

But apart from items such as silk cloth this invaluable trade route also carried one other item that was destined to have a profound effect on civilization across the globe. It was not something that was desired by people in the west but it came nonetheless. It was the plague, the Black Death.

Bubonic plague originated on the dry and arid plains of central Asia. It spread slowly westward, being carried in the goods of traders using the Silk Route. Spread by the fleas that normally lived on rats—carried now in bundles of cloth or rolls of carpet—the disease was undetectable until the symptoms began to hit the traders or the people who were buying from them.

By 1343 the Black Death had reached the Crimean Peninsula. From there it spread into Europe being carried, in the main, by merchant ships that traded with England, France and other western powers. By the time of its last major outbreak it is estimated that between 75 and 200 million people had died from the Black Death.

Living conditions that helped the disease flourish played a significant part in the story of the Black Death. However, the plague had been brought to the west by the Silk Route, a totally unexpected addition to the benefits that came through trade with China.

The one item that the Chinese did eagerly seize on was horses from the lands to the north of the Hindu Kush: "Much larger than those in China ... [they were] valuable military additions to the Chinese forces ... The breed, however, no longer exists, and is preserved only in paintings and sculptures."*

So protective of their land and ideas were the Chinese emperors that they built the Great Wall in order to defend their interests and keep foreigners out. As an entity, access along the Silk Road was always tenuous and the route was closed on many occasions—as when the Tibetans captured the area around the western end of the road in 678 BC.

The Mongol emperors reopened the route at the end of the 1200s but the decline or fragmentation of their empire saw the demise of the Silk Road. That demise, more than anything, clearly demonstrated that trade routes, wherever they ran and whoever ran them, needed strong government if they were to remain open and useful. With the growth of Islam and, in particular, the coming of the Turkish sultans, the Silk Road became almost permanently blocked by the 18th century.

---

* Carles Buenacas Perez, 'The Silk Road' in *National Geographic History*

The route of the old Silk Road. (fdecomite)

Such tenuous origins meant that while the people of the west were fascinated by and desirous of the produce that came along the Silk Road, actually getting their hands on it was difficult. That was where Marco Polo and his followers came in. Even so it was a slow and gradual process.

To begin with the opportunities for foreign investment were limited. There were other parts of the world with which to trade, in particular India where the East India Company was rapidly creating a monopoly. When China did finally open up to foreign investors it was the trade between India and China that marked the way.

During the 18th century the much-debated European concept of free trade began to rear its head in a particularly powerful and potent way. A sudden demand for tea, for silk and for luxury items such as books, fine porcelain and art meant that China and Chinese goods became immensely popular with the upper classes of Britain, France and the rest of the so-called civilized world.

In particular such goods were hugely important for trading nations like Britain. It might now seem bizarre, even criminal, but rather than adversely affecting the balance of payments, as a way of paying for such goods opium was introduced into China from British possessions in India. It was a clear government policy and the smoking of opium quickly became a passion, and an addiction, for the Chinese. By 1831 the opium trade was hugely significant: "The merchants realized that trade at Canton and Macao (where most of the merchants resided) represented only the tip of an immensely profitable iceberg. Already trade with China represented about 15 percent of total British overseas trade."[*]

The horrors of the drug were obvious to everyone who cared to look and eventually the Manchu Qing regime decided to try to curtail the selling and smoking of opium. There had been an imperial edict as early as 1729, forbidding the import and use of the drug. However, it had proved impossible to implement this order, particularly in the face of British pressure and determination. Now they were ready to try again. It was not their own people the imperial government had to convince, it was the foreign devils. Discussion and debate got them nowhere and, clearly, direct action was now called for.

In one recorded instance 20,000 cases of the drug were confiscated from a group of British government-sponsored traders and then destroyed. There were other seizures and in 1838, much to the fury both of local merchants and of government officials, a prominent British trader and opium dealer was expelled from Canton.

Powerless as they might ultimately prove to be, the officials of the Qing dynasty continued to challenge those controlling the trade. In March 1839 the Chief Superintendent for Chinese Affairs was compelled by the Chinese government to surrender all of the British opium stock. As Paul Hayes suggests, the British traders were furious, their pride hurt and, more importantly, their profit destroyed. The policy of restricting opium dealing and the resulting clamp-down on the trade caused near panic in the drawing rooms of England. Pressure was placed on Parliament, not so much by traders or even politicians but from their wives and families—petticoat government indeed. The posting of a British naval squadron to the seas off China had no effect: the Qing government was serious in its desire to restrict the opium trade, and it soon became clear to everyone that the matter would end badly.

As, indeed, it did. The highly laudable actions of the Qings culminated in a series of 'opium wars' between China and Britain, fought between 1839 and 1841 and again from 1858 to 1860, the British government under Lord Palmerston convincing themselves and the British public that they were in the right. In Victorian Britain, going to war over opium was a totally acceptable notion.

Victory for the British in the opium wars brought about the punitive treaties of Nanking (1842) and Whampoa (1844). The treaties, among other things, ceded Hong Kong to Britain and forced the Chinese to open up eight of their major ports to foreign control. Prior to this, trade with China had been possible only through Hong Kong and Macao.

---

[*] Paul Hayes, *The Nineteenth Century*

The Opium Wars

The story of the two opium wars between China and Britain is well known. Regardless of your stance—the very idea of Britain fighting a war to allow the trade in opium is an anathema to many—they were significant events that changed the course of history for China.

Fought between 1839 and 1842 and again from 1856 until 1860, the two wars were not foregone conclusions and involved serious military and naval encounters between the two sides. The result of the two conflicts was victory for Britain but it is in the effects that the wars left behind them, the sheer turmoil that descended across China, that the most significant results can be found.

For many years the Chinese economy had been one of the largest economies in the world, if not the largest. Yet the wars changed all that and following the second conflict the Chinese GDP (Gross Domestic Product, the total value of everything produced by a country) was reduced by half.

With the GDP in remission China was forced to trade with other parts of the world in order to bring goods and money into the country. In a nation that had been traditionally isolationist it was an alien move and the Qing dynasty was fatally weakened. This weakness was something that lay dormant for a number of years, but the Qings' days were numbered from this point on.

After the first opium war Hong Kong was ceded to Britain, in whose control the colony remained for many years. Apart from the humiliation of seeing a part of their country under the control of a foreign power, China lost millions of pounds which could and should have helped bolster the Chinese economy.

Under the terms of the same treaty China was forced to allow five of her biggest ports to become 'treaty ports' where Britain (and later other nations as well) could control trade and exploit the wealth that, again, should have remained in China. The ports were Shanghai, Canton, Ningpo, Foochow and Amoy, places that were to become well known in the tempestuous days ahead.

Perhaps the most significant result of the two wars came in the number of opium addicts in the country. By 1883 Britain and her compadres—the US and France—were sending 30,000 chests of opium from India to China every year. Soon there were between four and twelve million Chinese opium addicts, something that encouraged crime; with thousands of men and women of working age unable to work, this dealt a particularly heavy blow to the Chinese economy.

The analogy drawn by Harriet Ward in *World Powers in the Twentieth Century* is simple and compelling: imagine unchecked trading rights being granted in Liverpool, Southampton or Hull to nations like the USSR or the US, nations whose only claim to superiority was that they had defeated Britain in battle. Certain areas within the ports would be out of bounds to British citizens while American or Russian residents would be above the law both within and outside their concession areas. Russian and American companies would fix the import duty that the government could receive, with their merchants and traders free to travel anywhere in Britain.

Small wonder then, in a country that was as fiercely nationalistic as China, that the system of treaty ports was so bitterly resented. To the British, land hungry as ever, the acquisition of Hong Kong was merely the precursor to greater triumphs: "When the British acquired Hong Kong in 1841 ... one commentator likened the new colony to 'a notch cut in China as a woodsman notches a tree, to mark it for felling at a convenient opportunity'."*

The Chinese, of course, felt very differently. The loss of Hong Kong and the foreign concessions that followed it in other ports rankled like a festering sore. It was resentment that would, one day, erupt in violence and mayhem.

What the Chinese people were faced with were the twin shackles of imperialism and feudalism. It was a situation that the young, mainly middle-class thinkers of the time could see only too clearly. For perhaps the first time in the history of China such young people were suddenly geographically mobile; they had the time and the means to travel. On journeys abroad such people encountered foreign nations and foreign concepts such as democracy and human rights, things that they saw were clearly needed in China: "These young reformers in China and abroad were westernized in outlook but they were also strongly nationalist; they wanted to get rid of foreign influence in China and begin a programme of democratic reforms and economic development."†

The final years of the Qing dynasty were troubled and dangerous for many people in the country, not least the rulers themselves. They could not know it but what they were experiencing were the death throes of the empire. The Taiping Rebellion, which cost thousands of lives—some reports put the death toll in the hundreds of thousands—and lasted for fourteen years, broke out in 1850. It was one of the earliest united attempts, by the people rather than by an aspiring alternative dynasty, at overthrowing the traditional imperial system but resulted in the eventual defeat of the rebels.

A disastrous defeat in the First Sino-Japanese War of 1894 saw China lose territory and land in Manchuria as well as the island of Formosa and parts of Korea. It was

---

* James Morris, *Heaven's Command*

† Harriet Ward, *World Powers in the Twentieth Century*

a humiliating setback for the Qing dynasty and, perhaps more importantly, it marked the real beginnings of Japan's rise to dominance in the region, the true beginnings of the Japanese Empire, something that would grow like Topsy and would culminate in the campaigns in the Pacific theatre during the Second World War.

Resentment of foreigners, a feeling fuelled by military defeat and by perceived social injustices, had been growing steadily stronger for many years. For a while there was a reactionary movement in the country. The desire to revert to isolation, albeit with certain facets taken from the foreigners, was best summed up by the scholar and philosopher Feng Guifen, circa 1850: "What we have to learn from the Barbarians is only one thing—solid ships and effective guns."

Sun Yat-sen, the father of the nation.

When the unrest and unhappiness culminated in the Boxer Rebellion of 1900 the uprising took everyone by surprise—although there was no reason why it should have done. The simmering resentment had been clear for some time to anyone who cared to look. It was just that, like the British in India before the Mutiny, no one was prepared to accept that there was a problem. The uprising was sudden and violent, to all intents and purposes a revolt against foreign power and influence in China. Famous now for the siege of the International Legation at Peking, the rebellion seemed, for a while, to have a real chance of success. However, defeat of the Boxers, due to an almost unprecedented alliance of the eight international nations to have most control in the country, brought to an end the Chinese dream of freedom from the foreign powers. The Boxer Rebellion had begun soon after the emperor was removed from the throne by his aunt, the Dowager Empress Cixi who installed herself on the imperial throne in his place. Ruthless and determined to rid China of the foreigners, Cixi did not take an active part in the rebellion but her influence and scheming were undoubtedly a significant factor in the rising. She was clever and cunning, even managing to stay on the throne when the rebellion finally ended.

When she died in 1908 Cixi was in turn replaced by the next in line, the two-year-old infant Emperor Puyi. They did not know it at the time but Puyi was to be the last of the Manchu Qing dynasty and the last of the true Chinese emperors. His installation and inauguration marked the end of an era.

Left: The last emperor, Puyi, shown here as a young man.

Below: Execution of a Boxer rebel by the French. (Internet Archive Book Images)

The Boxer Rebellion

They are usually known as the Boxers because so many of them had participated in Chinese martial arts—boxing in particular. However, the real name of those who staged the Boxer Rebellion in 1899 and 1900 was the Righteous and Harmonious Fists or, sometimes, the Militia United in Righteousness. The Boxers—to stick with the commonly used term—were nationalists who were opposed to the influence of the western powers in China and also the effect of the increasingly numerous Christian missionaries.

The mood in China during the summer months of 1899 was, at best, fragile and fractious. There had been a severe drought for some time and this helped foment the growing anger of the Boxers. Violence broke out in Shandong and in the northern part of the country, riots that were clearly aimed at breaking the power of what were called 'the foreign devils'.

The real trouble, however, began in June 1900 when a large group of Boxers converged on Beijing—or Peking as it was then known—convinced that they were invulnerable to foreign weapons. Their aim was obvious as they marched chanting their slogan "Support the Qing government and exterminate the foreigners."

The foreigners, along with many Chinese Christians, sought refuge in the Legation area of Peking and a fifty-five-day siege began. When reports of an attempt to relieve the siege came to the attention of the Dowager Empress Cixi she changed her attitude, having initially been opposed to the Boxers, and on 21 June she issued an imperial decree declaring war on the foreign powers. The Imperial Army now joined the Boxers besieging the Legation in Peking.

A relief force made up of troops from eight different powers—the Eight-Nation Alliance comprising Britain, Russia, France, Japan, the US, Italy, Austria-Hungary and Germany (with the Netherlands in the wings)—was, initially, forced to turn back. Then they were reinforced by an extra 20,000 troops and the second attempt was successful. The Boxers and the Imperial Army were scattered. In the wake of the relief the capital and the surrounding countryside were plundered and there were widespread executions of anyone thought to have Boxer sympathies.

The cost to China of the Boxer Rebellion was enormous. The victorious foreign powers installed troops at Peking and 450 million taels of silver—the equivalent of $10 billion in today's money—was extracted as reparations. It all led to the ending of the Qing dynasty—costly indeed.

Boxers captured by the 6th US Calvalry. (Ralph Repo / Underwood & Co.)

Senior German officers during the Boxer Rebelleion. (M. Nössler)

Vice-Admiral Seymour loses face

When we write or think about the Boxer Rebellion it is invariably the fifty-five-day siege of Peking that comes to mind. But there was a lot more to the rebellion than that. One of the little known events involved the British vice-admiral Edward Seymour.

A multinational force under Seymour's command was sent to relieve the garrison at Peking, leaving Dagu on 10 June 1900. Seymour's force was comprised of 2,000 soldiers, sailors and marines, a large number of them being British. What was supposed to be a relief force for those holed up in the Legation, the army was far too small to achieve much success. The leadership was also lacking in skill and military prowess.

They travelled by train as far as Tianjin but then discovered that the Boxers had cut the railway line ahead of them, isolating Peking but, more importantly, keeping any sort of relief force away from the capital. Seymour's engineers tried, unsuccessfully, to repair the line but then discovered that the Boxers had now cut the railway tracks behind them. They could not go forward or and they could not go back. They were, effectively, trapped.

Admiral Seymour returning to Tianjin with his wounded troops and his tail between his legs. (*La Royale*, Jean Randier)

Seymour felt there was only one thing to do: they would march on Peking but at that moment the Boxers attacked. The battle of Lang-fang was fought on 18 June and resulted in a Boxer victory. Seymour was obliged to seek refuge in the Great Xigu Arsenal where he prepared to hold out for as long as he could. Alerted to Seymour's difficulties, a relief force of 1,800 Alliance troops was hastily assembled. Made up of troops from all eight Alliance nations, although principally Russian and British, they duly rescued the unfortunate Admiral but could do little to save his dignity.

Rather than face an outright defeat the Boxers slipped away to rejoin their comrades outside Peking. Seymour had lost sixty-two men killed in the affair while a further 228 were wounded.

A fish seller naps in the Old City. Apart from the electrical cables and plastic fish containers, little has changed in a century. (Christof Berger)

3. SUN YAT-SEN

At this point in the story the most significant figure in the history of early republican China, a man of considerable power, style and grace, rose to the fore. He was a compelling and dramatic character and his name was Sun Yat-sen. As a revolutionary, as a writer and as a political thinker, Sun was what every upsurge of popular emotion

Sun Yat-sen (seated)
and Chiang.

from an oppressed people always requires. He was a complex individual, a man of integrity with far-reaching ideas and ideals and yet someone who could also be utterly ruthless when the occasion demanded it.

Sun Yat-sen was born on 12 November 1866. His father, Sun Dacheng, owned a few acres of land but earned his living mainly as a tailor in Macao and as a journeyman porter and labourer. Born as Sun Wen or, genealogically, as Sun Deming, Sun Yat-sen did not adopt his more famous name until as an adolescent he went to school in Hong Kong.

He received most of his early education in Honolulu in Hawaii, living with his brother Sun Mei who had left China (like many young and ambitious men of the time) and made his home on the island. Hawaii was not then an American possession although, being so close to the western seaboard of the US, it was heavily influenced by American ideals and fashions.

By the time he graduated in 1882, Sun had taught himself English, becoming fluent in the language and gaining a firm insight into the values and culture of western Europeans. During his time in Hawaii Sun also came under the influence of American Christian brothers and was seriously considering being confirmed into the Christian faith.

His brother was unhappy at Sun's 'Christianization' and in 1883, when he was just seventeen years old, family pressure forced the young man to return to China. Sun accepted the decision with equanimity, being content to return to a homeland that he did not really know.

Once back in China Sun quickly found himself fascinated by the land, by the people and by what he now realized was the oppression—by the emperors and by the foreigners—under which his countrymen lived. He was not yet ready to do anything about it however, but found that his temper and indignation were becoming more and more potent. He also found himself in trouble when he and some friends in a fit of righteous anger deliberately destroyed a statue of the Beiji emperor god. The villagers who were worshipping the statue were incensed and would probably have killed the students if they could have got to them.

The group of young students, Sun included, had no option but to flee the country, the first of many periods that Sun Yat-sen spent in exile. He found sanctuary in Hong Kong where he remained for several years. Realizing the need for a qualification of some sort, Sun attended college in Hong Kong, finally graduating with a degree in medicine.

Sun's revolutionary attitude dates from this time in the British colony of Hong Kong, a place that was Chinese by right but which had for many years been a British enclave. He joined with other students of a revolutionary frame of mind, becoming

Sun Yat-sen and the Four Bandits.

one of The Four Bandits as they called themselves. It was a 'think tank' rather than a revolutionary agency and together the four young men discussed politics and solutions to world problems; in particular they discussed the situation back home in China.

After being baptized into the Christian church, Sun decided to abandon medicine and devote himself to transforming his homeland. From now on he was an implacable opponent of the imperial regime that had, in his opinion, misruled his country for many years. It was also, he felt, time that the foreign powers stopped bleeding China of revenue and either begin to put something back or else clear out for once and for all.

During these years Sun became involved with the Heaven and Earth Society, the Tiandihui, the Triads or Three Cooperating Organizations as they were sometimes known. Not in themselves a revolutionary body, he unashamedly used the society to fund his overseas travel and to garner support for future revolution. He became secretary of the Revive China Society, returned to his homeland and was devastated when China was defeated by Japan in the 1894/5 Sino-Japanese War. The Qings were, in the opinion of Sun and many others, entirely to blame for the defeat.

Railing against the inadequacies of the Qing dynasty, Sun was a central figure in what became known as the First Guangzhou Rebellion but when the uprising met with defeat the young revolutionary was forced, once again, into exile. This time

A disturbing postcard from 1900 simply entitled 'Chinese Execution'. Westerners pose on a beach after a recent execution, the beheaded victims at their feet. The similarity with Islamic State executions a century later is uncanny.

he found refuge in the American-held Philippines where he was instrumental in supplying weapons for local revolutionaries to use against the US. He had hoped to assist the Philippines to gain independence from the US but American victory in 1903 war for independence had ended this particular pipedream.

On 22 October 1900 Sun launched the Huizhou Uprising against the imperial leaders of China. Once again the revolution was unsuccessful and, for Sun Yat-sen, was followed by yet another period of exile, this time in Japan and Europe. At one stage he was detained for twelve days at the Chinese Legation in London after it was learned that the Chinese Secret Service had laid plans to kill him. The detention and the plot made him into something of a folk hero in Edwardian Britain.

In 1905 he joined with Chinese students then studying in Tokyo to form the revolutionary group Tongmenghui. Over the next few months the group planned and sponsored several small rebellions or uprisings in China but by the beginning of 1907 their attempts at undermining the Qing emperor had all failed disastrously.

Support for the Tongmenghui remained limited and even after two years, membership of the organization had still not managed to reach a thousand. However, the significance of the Tongmenghui lies not in what it achieved but in what it was to morph into in the years ahead.

In the face of repeated military failure Sun's position as one of the leaders of the Tongmenghui was in jeopardy. In particular, following the disaster of seven days' bitter and unsuccessful fighting around Friendship Pass during the Zhennanguan Uprising, his military leadership was put under severe scrutiny by his comrades. Sun suddenly found himself denounced. For someone like Sun who had pledged his whole life to displacing the imperial regime it was an unpleasant experience to have his activities, both political and social, questioned by the other members of the Tongmenghui. Sun Yat-sen fought off the challenge to his leadership—as he was to do several times—and continued to plan and lead further small (and unsuccessful) rebellions against the emperor.

It was ironic that when an uprising led by Huang Xing did finally succeed in overthrowing Puyi's regime, Sun was abroad and played no part in the venture. On hearing of the success of Huang's rebellion, however, Sun immediately headed back to China, arriving on 21 December 1911. He received a warm welcome from Huang and the other revolutionaries and just a week later Sun Yat-sen was elected provisional president of the new Chinese Republic.

The date set for the inception of the new republic was 1 January 1912 with the young Emperor Puyi being forced to abdicate his throne on 12 February. It was the end of two thousand years of imperial rule and a new era seemed to beckon for China.

Shortly afterwards, on 10 March, Sun Yat-sen himself stepped down as president and was replaced by Yuan Shikai, one of many warlords who still held power in China. Yuan had been an influential soldier during the last days of the Qing dynasty and was one of the few leaders to emerge from the Boxer Rebellion with any credit or dignity. He was, however, a dyed-in-the-wool conservative and saw no reason not to revert to the status quo—as soon as it was possible. People, both inside and outside the government, were well aware of his views.

Despite this, offering the presidency to Yuan was in many respects a shrewd political move as there were still elements of the army that supported the old Qing dynasty. Yuan had control of the military in the northern part of the country and in order to woo him and the army to their side, the revolutionaries had promised Yuan the position of president once the Qing court was finally removed from power.

Yuan Shikai, in impressive imperial garb.

Above: Yuan Shikai, warlord and self-proclaimed emperor, poses with his staff.

Left: Yuan Shikai, with his officers.

Sun did not object, seeing the sense of the move but he was worried by the persona and the personal traits of Yuan. They were certainly not characteristics he could approve of, even if his magnanimity had allowed the older man to attain power. Time, Sun knew, was not on Yuan's side.

One of the few significant decisions made by Yuan was to move the capital to Beijing. It was an arbitrary decision and, as far as many in the new regime were concerned, it showed the style of government that Yuan was intending to implement. Despite this, at Sun's behest telegrams were now dispatched to all of the provincial governments asking for representatives to be sent to Beijing, the new capital. There, Sun planned, the new National Assembly of the Republic of China was to be set up.

It was an early attempt at creating the democracy to which Sun had pledged his life. However, many of the revolutionaries were becoming increasingly wary of what they saw as the "vaulting ambition" of Yuan Shikai. Sun Yat-sen, resentful of any overtly dictatorial central authority, was prominent among the doubters. Like many insightful politicians and statesmen, he feared what Yuan might do next. Even at this early stage of the new republic it was obvious that trouble was brewing.

On 25 August 1912, Sun and Song Jiaren, a friend and colleague from the Tongmenghui, came together to form a new political party, the Kuomintang. The Tongmenghui had served its purpose: the new organization would now take things to the next level. The new party was commonly referred to as the KMT and was, by nature, opposed to both Communist ideology and the traditional imperialist views of people like Yuan Shikai. Sun, however, knew that he would need support from all sides of the political spectrum if he was ever going to achieve his desired ideal—the creation of a democratic and united China.

The new KMT was significantly nationalist in outlook and from the beginning had a strong popular base, winning 269 seats out of 596 at the 1912/13 elections for the National Assembly. The Nationalists (or, rather, the KMT) also took 123 out of 274 seats in the Senate. Quite how many of the electorate knew what they were voting for was another matter.

The term 'nationalism' in the context of modern politics has become something of a dirty word. However, in reality it relates to the practice of assisting your country or nation by uniting the people in one secure and solid self-governing state—which is not necessarily a bad thing to desire. Creating such a state was certainly what Sun Yat-sen wanted and was attempting to achieve in the years after the revolution of 1912.

Invariably after conflicts such as the First World War some nations, often the defeated ones, were left fragmented and disunited—hence the rise of strong nationalist parties such as the Fascists in Italy, Spain and Germany. They promised better times, they promised security, they promised strong leadership—and the masses fell into the trap of supporting ideologically flawed regimes where the emphasis was on the cult of the personality rather than programmes for the good of the people.

Nationalism in China, as advocated by Sun Yat-sen, was directly related to the injustices of the ruling system where, before 1912, all government was in the hands of what everyone thought of as the corrupt Manchu Qing dynasty. Similarly, most big business had been and still was the prerogative of foreigners. Everyone seemed to be benefitting—apart from the Chinese people themselves. Sun's nationalism had wanted to get rid of the Qings and then the foreigners. His aim was to create a series of democratic reforms where the beneficiaries would be the ordinary people of China. In that respect it was a much truer nationalism than that offered by people like Mussolini and Hitler.

Sun's position was not totally secure, however. The new republic had so far failed to unify China; in the words of Dan N. Jacobs, if anything they "had seemingly slipped backwards". Sun was only too aware that foreign help would be required if the country was ever going to unify and grow: "Even the United States, which Sun had repeatedly visited in order to seek support for his revolutionary movement, had not established itself without outside aid. To George Washington's side had come the

The upper reaches of the Yangtze river. (ChrisDing30)

On the Nanking road, Shanghai, c. 1920. (LoC)

French and their Marquis de Lafayette."* Sun Yat-sen was determined to find his own Lafayette. It was an idea that was contrary to the thinking of many, if not most, of the country's new rulers who retained the idea of isolationism that had kept China apart from other nations for too many years. For the moment, however, Sun Yat-sen could do little; the time was not yet ripe.

In the meantime there was the problem of Yuan to deal with. When Sun and Song Jiaren led a second revolution in July 1913, this time against Yuan Shikai, it was defeated by the vastly more powerful troops of Yuan's army and Sun was once more obliged to flee for safety. It seemed as if Sun Yat-sen was doomed to spend his life flitting in and out of exile but he was a man who held firm beliefs and was someone who counted personal inconvenience to be of little or no importance.

Song Jiaren, who was now leader of the Nationalist Party, could also have gone into exile but he stayed behind when Sun fled. It was a fateful decision as he was soon assassinated, probably on the orders of Yuan Shikai.

---

*   Dan N. Jacobs, article in *China in the 1920s*

In the chaos that followed Song Jiaren's murder, Yuan Shikai finally showed his true colours when he proclaimed an end to the republic and the return of the empire of China. As many had suspected and dreaded, he followed this up by announcing himself as the new emperor.

There was immediate uproar from those who had fought long and hard to free the country of imperial rule and anti-monarchy uprisings broke out all across China. In order to counter Yuan's imperial aims, the Nationalists duly proclaimed Sun as president of the Republic of China. It was a hollow gesture and not until 1917 did Sun feel safe enough to return and carry on the fight for Chinese unity. From exile he continued to denounce Yuan and plan for the day he could return.

In October 1915 Sun married Soong Ching-ling, one of three politically active and aware sisters. Despite her parent's opposition—he was twenty-six years her senior—Soong remained with Sun until his death and went on to a successful career in the Communist Party. She survived Mao's Cultural Revolution and died as a well-respected national figure. All of that was a long way ahead when she became Sun Yat-sen's second wife in the autumn of 1915.

Meanwhile, in China things were progressing apace—and not always in favour of Yuan Shikai. With province after province declaring against him Yuan finally began to realize the impossibility of his situation. Consequently, he resigned his self-proclaimed position as emperor in March 1916 after a 'reign' of just eighty-three days. He died a few months later—of natural causes. He was one of the few contemporary warlords to die peacefully, in his bed and with his boots off as American gunfighters might have said. Yuan had gone but the confusion and chaos he had created lived on.

The following year, 1917, the Russian Revolution took place and Tsar Nicholas II, the last of the Romanov emperors, was removed from his throne. Despite almost universal condemnation of the Bolshevik revolution, Sun Yat-sen was finally able to see a potential Lafayette in the shape of the new socialist government in Moscow. With Leon Trotsky already talking of exporting Communism worldwide, a partnership of some sort between Russia and China seemed a logical and mutually beneficial alliance. Sun was not a Communist and never would be. He was decidedly left wing in his beliefs but the Communist ideals were a step too far and were alien to his thinking. He was, however, not above using whatever means he could in order to achieve his ends—and that included the Communists.

He had already approached several western governments for help but had received no offers of aid, in hindsight a somewhat blinkered decision on the part of those governments. Taking advice and financial assistance from the revolutionaries in Russia and from the left-wing thinkers in China was, therefore, one of the few options left open to him.

Persuaded, in 1917, by the Allied powers to declare war on Germany, the Chinese revolutionary government was indignant when the Treaty of Versailles revealed the duplicity of the victorious western nations. German possessions in the Far East, possessions which the Chinese confidently expected—and some believed had actually been promised—to be gifted to them when Germany was defeated, went instead to Japan. It was more power to the burgeoning Japanese Empire and a wave of strikes and demonstrations erupted all across China.

The May 4th Movement, as the strikes were known, was accompanied by student riots and by a general boycott of Japanese goods. Sun Yat-sen's Kuomintang was at the forefront of the protest but so too were the country's Communists. Many of the Chinese people, already feeling let down and betrayed, eagerly listened to what the Communists had to say and they found their message of equality and land ownership more than a little appealing.

The Communist Party of China came into being in June 1921. The prime movers in creating the Party were Li Dazhao and Chen Duxiu but the young and, at that stage, inexperienced Mao Zedong was also one of the original functionaries. He was also one of the thirteen Party members who helped found the CPC mouthpiece newspaper *The Communist*. To begin with, however, the influence and the power of these left-wing radicals remained slight. Sun, while not above using their help, was determined that it would stay like that.

Nothing was simple or straightforward in a country as splintered and divided as China. Being able to play at politics was a crucial factor, something that Sun managed to do most successfully. Others were more direct in their approach and suffered by comparison.

On 10 October 1919 Sun Yat-sen resurrected the Kuomintang which had been banned by Yuan. By now, however, he had become convinced that the only hope for China lay in a military conquest that would obliterate all of the divergent powers and opinions. Following this 'cleansing', true democracy could then be finally installed.

As a precursor to this idea, in 1921 Sun established a military government in Guangzhou, with himself as Grand Marshal. He now began to cooperate ever more closely with the Communist Party of China (the CPC) and to involve himself in dialogue with the regime in Russia.

In January 1923 Adolph Joffre, a diplomat from the Soviet Union, came to Shanghai to confer with Sun Yat-sen. Three Russian agents had previously met with him and had formed a fairly negative opinion of the man and of the value of China as a communist ally. Joffre, a capable and well-respected diplomat who had been one of the prime movers behind the Brest-Litovsk Treaty that took Russia out of the First World War, was himself not convinced either: "In spite of their relatively

Soong Mei-ling, a later image, on the cover of *Liangyou* (*The Young Companion*) magazine. Soong was Sun Yat-sen's sister-in-law.

negative judgement of him, Moscow was convinced that Sun could be useful to the revolution in China. Besides, the pressure on the Comintern to become involved in the east had grown."*

The outcome of Joffe's meeting with Sun was that the Soviet government would agree to provide military and financial aid to Sun's Nationalists. The agent and provocateur Mikhail Borodin was sent to China as an adviser, along with several other military experts.

Borodin came from a Jewish family in what is now modern-day Belarus. He became a Bolshevik in 1903 but two years later went into exile in the US. He returned to Russia after the November Revolution of 1917 that brought Lenin to power and began

---

* Jacobs

to work at extending Communist influence across the world. Dedicated to his role, Borodin was happy to become adviser and mentor to the Chinese Communists.

He was also committed to Lenin's idea of democratic centralism and was given the full support of the Comintern. How long such support would last in an ever-changing political maelstrom like post-revolutionary Russia was a different matter. In the meantime, Borodin was instrumental in creating a united front between Sun Yat-sen's Nationalists and the Communist Party of China. It was a pragmatic approach that seemed to work—at least for a while.

Borodin was the man who arranged the various shipments of arms to China and helped to create both the Peasants Training Institute (where Mao Zedong served) and the Whampoa Military Academy where both Chiang Kai-shek and his rival Wang Jingwei were soon to take up posts. For several years he remained an influential figure in China, a valuable link between Sun Yat-sen and the Comintern in Moscow.

Chiang and a chest full of medals.

In return for Russian help Sun Yat-sen agreed that Chinese Communists would be allowed to join the KMT. However, they would only be admitted to the Kuomintang as individuals. There was to be no acceptance of, or alliance with, the Communists as a bloc. For Communists who were interested in joining the KMT, Sun stated, there would be an expectation that, regardless of their personal beliefs, they would support KMT ideology and adhere to the party discipline. Lenin and, later, Stalin seemed to concur with Sun's decision and many Chinese Communists were duly admitted. Sun had clearly mapped out the expectation both from himself and from the Kuomintang. There was, at that stage, no reason to suppose that the Russians were operating on anything but genuine sentiment. It was always a rather naïve expectation. There was, from the start, an understanding from the Russians that the Communist members of the KMT should "conquer from within" and almost immediately there was conflict between the left and right wings of the party. It was a conflict that was to have dire consequences in the years ahead.

Early in 1925 Sun Yat-sen, assisted by Mikhail Borodin, began planning what became known as the Northern Expedition. This was in line with his thinking about uniting the country after military conquest—prior to the creation of a truly democratic nation. In Sun's scheme there was to be a military advance on a broad front, an assault that would take out the enemies of the new Republic, particularly the warlords who still held sway in the northern part of China.

Sun installed one of his protégées, Chiang Kai-shek who, along with Wang Jingwei, had been instrumental in developing the Whampoa Military Academy, as commandant of what now became the National Revolutionary Army (NRA). It was an important appointment, one that was to have a significant effect on China for many years.

Despite failing health Sun travelled extensively in the final months of his life, making speeches and reinforcing his Three Principles by which he had always hoped to unite China: nationalism, democracy and a just society for all. He was well aware that the vast majority of Chinese were illiterate and that democracy was, at that stage, beyond their understanding. It would, therefore, require an extensive period of education before the dream became reality.

His slogan 'Freedom, Progress and the Welfare of the People' was chanted wherever he went and the ordinary Chinese workers could see potential progress and benefit in his beliefs. Part of Sun's concept of improving the welfare and livelihood of the people consisted of redistributing land so that the men and women who worked the fields would be the ones to benefit rather than absentee landlords. It was not quite Communism but it was close.

Laudable as these principles might be, when the euphoria of his words had passed, there was little real substance to the promises. They were a dream, an ideal and by the time of Sun's death they were still little more than a distant wish for the people of China.

Sun had been suffering from cancer for some time and despite various treatments, including traditional Chinese medicines, nothing seemed able to halt the disease. He died from liver cancer on 12 March 1925, mourned and revered as 'the father of the nation'. His tragedy was that he died too soon, before his work was finished. Sun's death left a vacuum and his two closest associates, Chiang Kai-shek and Wang Jingwei, immediately became involved in a struggle for power. They were already men of influence, each with a definite idea of where they saw China going and of their role in the process.

Divergent opinions and two power-

Chiang and his wife, Soong Mei-ling.

ful individuals who were intent on getting their own way, inevitably left China in a delicate position where control could go either of two ways—but whichever of the two contenders for Sun Yat-sen's throne emerged victorious, one thing was certain: pain and suffering would undoubtedly be the lot of the ordinary people.

The Northern Expedition which Sun Yat-sen had been talking about and planning for some time would provide both would-be leaders with the opportunity to press their claims for control of the KMT and, as a natural consequence, of the country. Whoever was victorious the lucky general would not only gather kudos for himself, he would also establish a power base that would be unlikely to be beaten down. Everything, it seemed, depended on the long-delayed Northern Expedition.

4. THE NORTHERN EXPEDITION

It was not just Chiang Kai-shek and Wang Jingwei who had designs on the leadership of the KMT. There were several senior members of the Kuomintang who wanted and felt that they deserved the role as Sun's successor. Prominent among these were Liao Zhongkai and Hu Hanmin, both of whom had significant power bases and a large number of supporters.

The two main contenders to fill the empty space left by their leader's untimely death, however, were Chiang Kai-shek and Wang Jingwei. They were both, in their own way, protégées of Sun and while he had not gifted either with the succession, they both had expectations of power and position. Inevitably, along with Hu and Liao they now became antagonists.

The field was narrowed somewhat when Liao was assassinated and Hu was imprisoned, implicated in the murder of his opponent. Such murders and goings-on were typical of China at this time. It was a dangerous place to make a political career. However, the demise of Liao and Hu left just Chiang and Wang to compete for Sun's place.

Wang Jingwei, a formal photograph.

Chiang Kai-shek was born to a middle-class family on 31 October 1887 in Xitou, some thirty miles from Ningbo. He lost his father when he was just eight years old and perhaps as a consequence was something of a mischievous child. He once thrust a pair of chop sticks down his throat to see how far they could go. The chop sticks became stuck and he nearly died as a result.

Educated at the Military College in Japan, Chiang was ambitious and determined, so ambitious in fact that he divorced his wife and cast out his concubines in order to marry Soong Mei-ling, the sister of Sun's widow. This family connection, Chiang thought, would give him kudos and acceptance from the Chinese people, particularly from the supporters of Sun Yat-sen. He also converted to Christianity—at his wife's behest—again in the hope that it would bring him further acceptance.

The three Soong sisters in their youth; from left: Ai-Ling, Ching-Ling and Mei-Ling.

Soong Mei-ling *aka* Madame Chiang Kai-shek, broadcasting on behalf of her husband.

The relationship between Chiang and Soong Mei-ling was long lasting and, as he had hoped, entirely beneficial to him. Educated in America, Soong spoke perfect English—albeit with a Georgian accent—and was both personable and physically attractive. She was the youngest of the three Soong sisters, all of whom married important statesmen and officials of the Chinese government. During her time with Chiang, Soong filled a number of different roles in the KMT. She was, very clearly, an attractive and acceptable figure, both to the people of the western nations and to the Chinese.

Chiang's first mentor had been Chen Qimei, a supporter of Sun Yat-sen. When a dispute arose between Chen and Tao Chen-Chang, a long-time opponent of Sun, Tao took refuge in Shanghai's local hospital. Chiang was sent to negotiate and Tao was murdered. Whether Chiang was directly responsible or not he was certainly part of the murder plot. It showed his ruthless streak and when, in due course, Chen Qimei was himself assassinated by agents of Yuan Shikai, Chiang succeeded him as leader of the Chinese Revolutionary Party in Shanghai.

Even at this relatively early stage of his career it was obvious that Chiang held views that were somewhat opposed to the democratic and rather idealistic socialist ideas of Sun Yat-sen. Sun had organized the KMT along Communist lines but had not been a Communist himself, preferring to stay outside or above the left-wing machinations of the party.

Chiang had little time for Communist ideals. They held no appeal for him, either as an individual or as the leader of his party. He was an altogether more direct and autocratic leader who leaned towards authoritarianism rather than the left-wing policies advocated by his mentor. Military conquest followed by social democracy was his averred idea, a variation of Sun's three steps to democracy: military rule, political tutelage and, finally, constitutional rule.

Wang Jingwei was born as Wang Zhaoming in 1883 but was always more widely known by his pen name of Jingwei. A close associate of Sun Yat-sen's over the last twenty years of his life, Wang was at first a member of the left wing of the KMT but he gradually became disenchanted with the Communists and eventually his political affiliations veered sharply to the right. That, however, was in the future, long after his leadership contest with Chiang Kai-shek was over.

Originally sponsored and funded by the Qing dynasty, Wang was sent to Japan for his education but he soon came to view the imperial Qings with distrust. The imperial regime was, he felt, directly responsible for holding back the development of his country and in 1910 he devised a plot to assassinate the regent governing China in the name of the infant Puyi. The plot was discovered, Wang was put on trial, found guilty and duly sentenced to death.

Wang's courage at his trial, and in the face of his potential execution, made such an impression on the regent that his sentence was reduced to life imprisonment.

Zhou Shouyi, the influential editor of *Liangyou* (*The Young Companion*) magazine, seen here in 1927. Aimed at the younger, trendier middle class, he tried to keep the publication apolitical, but was ultimately forced through circumstances to focus on the more martial aspects of China in the 1920s and 1930s. He relocated to Hong Kong just before Mao assumed power.

As with so much of Chinese history in these years this was a dreadful mistake—for the imperialists, at least.

Released after the 1911/12 revolution, Wang became a major player in the Tongmenghui and Kuomintang. If anything he was more supportive of Sun than Chiang Kai-shek ever was and, together with Chiang, he remained a powerful figure in China in the period following Sun's death.

The Northern Expedition, the attack on the northern warlords for which Sun Yat-sen had long plotted and planned had been severely delayed, not least because of Sun's illness and death. Sun had appointed Chiang Commander of the National Revolutionary Army and as such he was considered to have the final say in matters concerning the military. After considerable planning and gathering together of troops he finally launched the expedition on 27 July 1926.

The aim of the Northern Expedition had always been to eliminate the warlords who still ruled with almost medieval authority over large parts of China. Sun had always believed that if this was done effectively it would go a long way in uniting the country. Neither Chiang nor Wang disagreed with this analysis although each retained his own agenda and ideas for the implementation of unity when it was finally achieved.

Chiang's plan was simple but effective. His forces would be organized into three divisions or armies that would each push northward towards the Yangtze River. The river effectively cut China in two and many of the country's main trading ports were located on this vital lifeline. It made control of the Yangtze crucially important: as Chiang knew, he who controls the Yangtze controls China.

With this in mind, each of the three assault groups would operate as individual armies and each of them, therefore, had its own objective. Overall, however, the three objectives dovetailed into one: get to the Yangtze River.

Wang Jingwei would advance in the west, aiming to attack and take Wuhan. Chiang's friend and supporter General Bai Chongxi was to advance on Shanghai in the east while Chiang himself would take the central route and head for Nanking.

From the outset there were immediate successes on all three fronts as the three armies swept every opponent before them. The province of Guangdong in the southeast, home to Canton and Hong Kong, and the large ports of Hunan and Jiangxi were soon in Nationalist hands and before the end of 1926, just a few months after the expedition had been launched, almost half of China was under the control of the Revolutionary Army.

Chinese women labourers weeding a wealthy foreigner's lawn in Shanghai, early 20th century. (Frank and Frances Carpenter Collection / LoC)

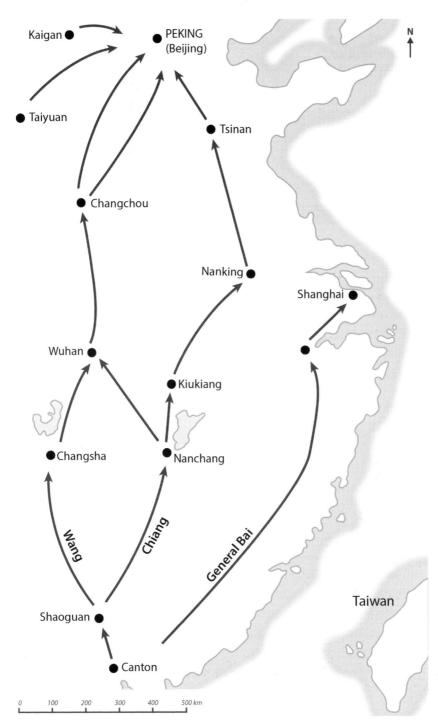

The Northern Expedition.

In many cases the three armies did not even have to fight. The warlords were not stupid and most of them knew that their time was up: "Unwanted, outnumbered and out gunned, many of the warlords capitulated and agreed to align with the Kuomintang."*

It was not long before Shanghai came under direct threat from General Bai's column. His forces pierced the city's defences on 18 March, the garrison commander handing over the military plans for the city's defence before he inexplicably left for home—where he was duly executed. After that it was only a matter of time. However, Bai was delayed just long enough in taking Shanghai for the local Communists to call a strike and attempt to set up a Soviet style council in the city.

Fiercely anti-Communist by nature, Bai ordered his troops to put down the strike. It was not easy as the Communists had managed to gain a great deal of public support and for some days there was a considerable amount of disruption in various parts of the city. For what seemed like an eternity gangs of youths roamed the streets, throwing stones at foreigners wherever they could find them—the tennis courts and bowling green in the French legation were one particularly attractive target. But it was more nuisance value than real opposition and by the end of the month Bai was firmly in control of the city: "As the *North China Daily News* noted, 'It would be a mistake to say that the Northern resistance collapsed; none was ever offered' ... One rare act of resistance was by the Russian armoured train which moved along the track at walking pace, firing at the southerners before its crew finally gave up."†

The use of armoured trains—or railway guns as they were more usually known—had been common since the days of the American Civil War when heavy artillery was mounted on flatbed railway trucks and taken to wherever they were needed. Mounted on semi-circular tracks, the guns could fire in all directions and, to the people of the target area, were terrifying. Experience was later to show that such weapons were both expensive and vulnerable to air attack but in a conflict like Chiang's Northern Expedition and the capture of Shanghai such considerations did not matter.

The Russian Red Army had made particular use of such weapons in their civil war against the Whites and with good railway connections between the Soviet Union and China the Russian railway gun could be moved swiftly to the front. It was, for a while at least, an effective terror weapon. Its value, however, was short lived.

Nationalist forces moved into Nanking the day after Shanghai fell and from the beginning the city provided a rather different problem for Chiang Kai-shek. What happened there has since become known as the Nanking Incident.

---

* alphahistory

† Fenby

By 23 March the NRA forces under Chiang's overall command were rapidly approaching the strategically important port. Compared to the troops of the local warlord Zhang Zangchang, the NRA soldiers were vastly superior, both in numbers and quality. Realizing the danger he was facing, Zhang Zangchang decided that discretion was certainly the best part of valour and ordered his troops to abandon the city and retreat.

As a treaty port a large force of British and American cruisers and destroyers was stationed in the Yangtze delta, close to Nanking. Their purpose was to protect the city's international settlement from attack but when the moment came the ships, their crews, along with most of the international community, were taken totally by surprise.

On the morning of 23 March troops of the NRA were in the city before anyone realized what was happening. It was only when the crews of the waiting warships saw smoke beginning to curl above the houses that they realized the danger. Looting and rioting had broken out in the densely packed streets where the Chinese workers lived and in the international cantonments. European and American citizens were at risk and everyone now realized that action had to be taken.

The origin of the troubles was, at this stage, unknown. Rumour was already rife however: the fires had been started by deserters from Zhang's retreating forces, the local Communists were to blame, the fires had been set by units of the National Revolutionary Army. The soldiers of the NRA came mainly from the Communist-heavy 6th Army that was now entering the city unopposed and to many of the terrified

A typical gunboat on the Yangtze.

HMS *Ladybird* off Shanghai. (USN)

members of the international community there was nothing to choose between soldiers, Communists and the leftovers of Zhang's retreating army. In these early moments of the rioting all things were possible.

The extent of army involvement has never been totally clear but it is highly unlikely that the Communist units in the force would have allowed such an opportunity to pass without at least attempting to take advantage. It remains guesswork.

Over the next few hours fist fighting, shooting and stone throwing became endemic as rioting Chinese ran unchecked through the city. J. E. Williams, the American vice president of Nanking University, was killed and the Japanese consul barely managed to escape with his life. Both the British and the US consulates were ransacked by the crowd, the port doctor and the harbour master shot dead and a French and Italian priest were murdered.

Within a few hours British and US warships had pulled in, close to shore. The British flagship, the old cruiser HMS *Vindictive*, was accompanied by no fewer than eight destroyers as well as by minesweepers and the river gunboats *Aphis* and *Cricket*. The smaller gunboats and destroyers were of more value than the *Vindictive* which, by the nature of her design, was more cumbersome and deeper of draft. The US Navy had five destroyers and even the Italians and French sent in gunboats to rescue their nationals.

Chinese troops with field gun.

Targeted by Chinese snipers the international residents fell back to a house high on Socony Hill. In an effort to protect the fleeing civilians US and British warships opened fire with their heavy guns before sending marines and troops ashore to evacuate the beleaguered civilians. Many of the civilians escaped from the house on Socony Hill by creating ropes from silk clothing and shimmying down from the windows.

The Allied ships were fired on by snipers, the attacking Chinese forces using rifles, machine guns and field pieces, as the destroyers, their job done, turned away from the shore and headed downstream. Their decks were crowded with refugees, and it needed machine-gun fire and high-explosive shells from all of the warships to keep the NRA at bay. Between them the USS *Noa* and *Preston* alone fired 67 rounds of high-explosive shells at the Chinese batteries on the shore. The Allied vessels sailed on downstream leaving Nanking behind them. By then the town was battered and littered with shell craters.

Approximately forty people were killed in the Nanking Incident—Chinese, British, American, French and Japanese—before Cheng Qian, the local NRA commander, was able to reign in his troops. Afterwards the NRA, now in possession of Nanking, blamed deserters from Zhang's army and the Communists within their own forces for the incident.

Despite the Nanking Incident Chiang Kai-shek could feel relatively pleased with his progress. By the end of March 1927 the three major targets had been taken and were

Wang Jingwei.

now under his control. Only at Wuhan on the western flank of the assault did there appear to be difficulties—and they were not problems that Chiang Kai-shek had foreseen.

On 27 January 1927 Wang Jingwei, to great applause and loud fanfare from the people of the town, had ridden into Wuhan in some style. He looked and felt like a conqueror and it is more than possible that the adulation went to his head. Over the next few weeks, as Chiang was dealing with the fallout from the Nanking Incident, the loose alliance between Chiang and his colleague Wang Jingwei began to go awry.

Advised by Mikhail Borodin and by leading members of the CPC, Wang saw an opportunity for himself. He had no love for the Communists but Borodin convinced him that this was a chance he could not miss. If he really wanted to displace Chiang and sit firmly on Sun's 'throne', Borodin counselled, he would need to act now. Wang agreed, guessing that Borodin was playing something of a double game but, at the same time, knowing that this was probably going to be his only chance of displacing Chiang. The CPC still recognized Beijing as the capital of the country; whatever happened in Wuhan affected only the left wing of the KMT.

Time was of the essence and after only limited consideration Wang declared that the Nationalist government had now been moved from Beijing to Wuhan. More importantly, he said, he was in control of the government and of the military forces in the city. He seemed, Chiang thought, to be declaring independence from him and from the rest of the KMT.

Chiang Kai-shek, knowing that this could not be allowed to go unchallenged, immediately laid plans to turn away from Nanking and march on Wuhan. A violent clash between Chiang and Wang now seemed almost inevitable.

Chiang's army was immeasurably stronger than his opponent's, however, and Wang soon realized that his outnumbered forces would stand no chance against a determined and angry Chiang Kai-shek. He immediately began to regret his actions. A telegram from Stalin, urging the Communists in Wuhan to form a People's Army, did not help matters. It served only to alarm Wang even more. Wang was no

Mikhail Borodin, left, 'advising' his Chinese colleagues.

coward—his behaviour at his treason trial many years before had proved that—but he was also a realist and knew when a cause was lost. There would, he knew, be other opportunities in the future.

Consequently, in the face of a potential attack by Chiang's Nationalist troops, Wang capitulated and pledged allegiance to his rival. It meant the end of a ridiculous situation where China, for a brief period, had actually had three separate capitals: Beijing with the Communists in control, Wuhan with the left wing of the KMT dominating affairs and Nanking where Chiang's right-wing Nationalists held sway.

The Ninghan Separation, as the split between the two leaders later became known, ended when, a few weeks later, Wang left China and sought refuge in Europe. He would return but, for the moment, it appeared as if Chiang Kai-shek had been victorious in his desire to become the successor to the Father of the Nation, Sun Yat-sen.

*

By now Chiang and several of the more significant members of the Kuomintang had become alarmed about the activities of the Communists within their ranks. Up until now the KMT had tolerated their presence. It was, after all, what Sun Yat-sen had wanted. But the behaviour both of the left-wing members of the KMT and of the Communists was, many felt, now spiralling out of control. It was not just their involvement in the Nanking Incident, serious as that had been, or Wang's 'UDI'—his unilateral declaration of independence—in Wuhan. If the disruption had stopped there then the situation might have been bearable.

The Canton–Hong Kong Strike of the previous year had given everyone a clear indication of the strength of the Communists—and of their intentions. The strike had lasted from June 1925 until October 1926. It had been a direct result of British colonial policemen, most of them Sikhs under the command of British officers, shooting dead nine Chinese demonstrators. Whatever its causes, the Canton strike escalated and the situation in the Hong Kong area was soon out of control. Within days the dispute had grown into one of the most significant labour stoppages in the history of British imperialism.

Wu Tieh-cheng (centre) during the Northern Expedition. Wu later became the mayor of Shanghai and vice premier and foreign minister of the country. He fled to Taiwan in 1949, where he died in 1953.

When Communist officials in the Guangdong region offered free train passage to anyone who would like to come to the area to assist the strikers over 250,000 supporters flocked to Canton and Hong Kong to help. The offer of free train tickets probably contributed to the stampede but, more than that, it showed the power of the working classes if someone was able to harness their enthusiasm and energy.

Soon the city of Hong Kong was in serious difficulties. The colony's trade fell by half, the economy of the whole area was paralyzed and the British government was soon obliged to loan £3 million in order to shore up the economy and the government itself. Although the strike was mainly over by the end of 1925, a boycott of British goods ran on well into 1926 and continued to cause major problems.

If this, Chiang and his comrades in the KMT decided, was an indication of the strength of the Communists then their potential to cause trouble was vast. The Nanking Incident and further demonstrations in Shameen (Shamian) were proof positive of the continued desire of the CPC to disrupt the Nationalist plans. In fact, the CPC had already decided on a new plan of action, one that was far closer to the nightmare that Chiang dreaded. Guided by the indefatigable Mikhail Borodin, they had come to the conclusion that the Canton–Hong King strike had been effective and good for the party. But if they wanted to grow even stronger the CPC now needed to extend their activities beyond Canton and Hong Kong.

Borodin knew that if the revolution—and by that he meant the Communist revolution—was ever going to succeed in China it would need more backing than the strikers in Canton had received from the Comintern in Moscow. He regarded the strike and its ramifications as a missed opportunity but, compared to what he had in mind, it was still a minor altercation.

Canton might well be "a tower of Babel in which it is possible to get completely lost" but, more importantly, Borodin believed—and convinced the Soviets to believe—that a different approach was now needed. The KMT must act swiftly: "[They should] move their centre of revolution to a new area where the inhabitants were more susceptible to radical changes ... the Chinese leaders could conveniently leave South China under the guise of the 'northern expedition'."[*]

Now, as Chiang's march northward continued, it had become increasingly clear that the hidden agenda of the CPC was finally emerging. In their desire to promote social revolution among the peasants and the working classes of the country, direct action had replaced surreptitious prompting. It seemed that nothing could stop the Communists pushing the boundaries of what had, by then, become acceptable to the Kuomintang. Under CPC prompting peasants across the country had begun to take

---

[*]   Jacobs

the law into their own hands. Many of them now began attacking their landlords and when the premises of more and more foreign capitalists—an anathema to the CPC—were sacked or burned, foreign governments began considering their options. Many of them were close to military intervention, sending in troops and warships in order to protect their citizens and what they saw as their rights.

The arrival of more foreign troops in China was not something Chiang wanted. He knew that no matter how strong his armies might be they would be no match for the ships, guns and tactics of countries like the US and Britain. His army was made up, principally, of riflemen and sharpshooters. They did possess a few artillery pieces and machine guns, weapons that were more than enough to take care of the warlords and their bands of brigands but they could not begin to compete with the advanced soldiery of the Allied nations.

At the end of the day it came down to a simple decision: how far left did Chiang and his colleagues intend the revolution to go? The Soviets had always wanted to convert Chiang to Communism. Failing that, they had hoped to cause enough disruption to prevent him from uniting China before the CPC became strong enough to offer him a direct challenge.

In line with that idea, the Comintern in Moscow had happily concurred with the advice of Adolph Joffre and given Soviet assistance to the CPC. Leon Trotsky, in particular, was totally committed to the concept of worldwide revolution and his support was almost automatic. Stalin, who had clawed his way to power after Lenin's death, took a more cautious approach. For him it was a case of favouring the growth of socialism in one country—Russia—before exporting the Communist dream to the rest of the world.

Trotsky had warned the Comintern that Chiang would, ultimately, betray his Communist partners in the CPC and in Moscow. He even went so far as to advise members of the Chinese Communist Party to develop their own revolutionary programme rather than rely on the loyalty and support of Chiang Kai-shek. Stalin simply shrugged off the warning: "We can use Chiang as a peasant uses his horse. We can use him to lead the battle against the imperialists." Trotsky clearly had a better and more realistic view of Chiang than his leader. Or perhaps he was just more cynical. Trotsky certainly knew his man, realizing that Chiang had only two concerns: what was best for China and what, ultimately, was best for him.

On 21 March 1927 China's Labour Union, probably the largest trade union in the country and an organization that was backed by the CPC, suddenly implemented a general strike in the treaty port of Shanghai. The port was the industrial heartland of what was still a mainly rural country and, as such, it had a significance that was clear to everyone. It was the very scarcity of heavy industry in China that made Shanghai such a vital hub in the country's economy and the idea of workers from

Arresting Communist strikers.

the city going on strike filled the political leaders—apart from the Communists—with little enthusiasm.

Although it started before the Nanking Incident it was some time before Chiang heard the news. When it did finally filter through what had now become a rather fractured and damaged communication system he immediately left for Shanghai where, after travelling downriver by gunboat, he arrived on 26 March.

The strike was a mammoth enterprise, with over half a million city workers involved. The virtual seizure and closing down of Shanghai by workers immeasurably strengthened the position of the CPC and gave them control of the local government. This was an opportunity they were not going to miss and they immediately demanded the withdrawal of the military and naval forces of the foreign powers. It seemed like a logical move but, following the recent events in Nanking, the targeted foreign powers were now in a state of near hysteria: "As tension mounted, the treaty powers rushed warships and troops to Shanghai and the British Foreign Office even considered the possibility of occupying the city. For some time, it appeared as if foreign intervention was imminent."*

It is hard to know exactly what the Labour Union expected to achieve, both from the strike and from the demand to remove foreign troops. Apart from a response to the standard strikers' call for better working conditions, more pay and other generic issues, there was nothing really at stake. In many respects it was just a flexing of

---

* Tien-wei Wu in *China in the 1920s*

muscles, a desire to cause problems and cripple the government of the area, much as the Canton–Hong Kong strike had done so recently. Beyond that there seemed little to be gained. As it turned out, the strike was to have an effect that nobody, not the Labour Union, not the CPC, not even the Kuomintang, could ever have thought possible. Only Chiang knew what it might lead to and, for the moment at least, his decisions and future action remained locked within his head.

When he entered the city even Chiang was amazed at the strength of the Communists who were now virtually in total control. Among everything else they had achieved, they had also created a series of powerful workers militias, possibly not as well trained and organized as Chiang's forces but fuelled and driven by enthusiasm and by belief in the Communist ideal. The strikers, who were growing more militant by the hour, expected support from the Kuomintang and the Nationalist Party. At public meetings and demonstrations they demanded it.

Chiang, newly arrived, found himself in a difficult situation. The situation was intolerable and his determination to settle, once and for all, with the Communists grew stronger by the minute. He knew he would have to act: it was just a question of when he would do it. And, to begin with, he was not sure if he was powerful enough.

He had moved quickly once he heard the news of the general strike and most of his soldiers were either still in Nanking or, following in his wake, on their way to Shanghai. He now realized that he was in a much weaker position than he would have liked, perhaps even fatally so. Not only were his troops few in number, the opposition seemed to be in the ascendency: "He had only 3,000 troops in the city, including some former warlord soldiers whose reliability was uncertain ... Radical students demanded his removal, and workers waved banners declaring 'Overthrow Chiang Kai-shek'."* Armed groups of Communists openly paraded in the streets, jeering and shouting, and Chiang was informed that a specially inaugurated Communist committee was, even now, planning to take control of the city before his Nationalist units began arriving in strength. They were, he was told, drawing up lists of people to be assassinated. Of one thing he could be sure: his name would be on more than one of those lists.

Realizing that the situation was, potentially at least, dangerous and possibly even fatal, Chiang decided to proceed cautiously. He was, to begin with, vocal in his praise of the workers and what they had achieved. It was what the Communists and trade union workers wanted to hear and, for a short while they were somewhat placated.

Wang Jingwei, in the days before he fled the country, had also made the trip to Shanghai. He appeared in the city on 5 April, seeming as ever to be running in the wake of Chiang Kai-shek. It was not an analogy that the ambitious Wang would

---

* Fenby

Right: Chiang on the cover of *Liangyou*.

Below: In the Caucasus, 1927. From left: Mikhail Borodin, Soong Ching-ling, Wang Renda and Deng Yanda.

have recognized. Wang and the CPC leader Chen Duxiu promptly issued a joint statement, reaffirming the idea of cooperation between the KMT and the Communist Party of China. Yet again, that was what the strikers wanted to hear. Not Chiang, however. He desperately pleaded with Wang to desist from such inflammatory declarations and to help him eliminate the Communist influence from the KMT. His appeals had no effect. Wang left Shanghai after just one day and was soon in exile in Europe.

For several days there was a stalemate. Shanghai, the centre of the general strike and stoppage, was at a standstill, apart from the groups of idle workers who now paraded up and down the city streets. They carried banners, many of them denouncing Chiang Kai-shek and the Nationalists. Little business was being done in the face of increasingly rowdy workers' meetings.

It was a time of tense excitement and potential, at least for the strikers, but even they could sense that over the city there hung a pall of anxiety. There was one overarching concern, one question on everyone's lips: what would Chiang Kai-shek do? And, for the more militant members of the CPC, the main question was whether they could dispense with him before he did the same to them.

Meanwhile, in Wuhan, still a hotbed of left-wing activists, Chiang was condemned for what the Communists in the city saw as his unilateral actions. Wang might have

Troops barricaded in one of the legations.

gone but the Communist leaders of the community were adamant that Chiang Kai-shek must pay for his temerity. At its heart was the old cult of the personality, the case of the man growing bigger than the cause. As far as the Chinese were concerned the cult of the personality had begun with Sun Yat-sen. It was not necessarily something he had deliberately fostered or created but it was always there in all his dealings with the people. In the eyes of many he was the saviour, the man who had been put upon the earth to bring China, kicking and screaming maybe, into the modern world.

In the years after Sun's death both Chiang Kai-shek and Wang Jingwei had tapped into this powerful emotion, unashamedly playing to the adulation of their followers. It would be wrong to say that they enjoyed it but both men saw the value of a loyal, even fanatical, following and were not slow to exploit it. The only trouble with personal loyalty has always been the level of antipathy and hatred it brings out in the opposition. Viewed coldly, after the ending of Wang's thrust for power, the Wuhan Communists finally felt able to condemn the man they saw as the main proponent of the cult of the personality: Chiang Kai-shek. The power of individual personalities was not what Communism was about—at least not in theory.

As a result the city's Central Committee now ordered that Chiang should be stripped of his position as Commandant of the National Revolutionary Army. It was a hollow gesture, a statement or an order that could not possibly be followed up or achieved. But despite the toothless edict from Wuhan, it did show that relations between Chiang and the Communists had reached an all-time low. It was a situation that was now never going to change, right to the end of what soon became the civil war, right to the end of Chiang's life.

Degrading, denouncing and criticizing Chiang was also a rather foolish stance for the Wuhan Communists to take. It was an action that was fuelled by self-delusion and by what might be regarded almost as a death wish. The Chinese Communist Party seemed, at this time, to be totally unaware that they were playing with fire, not realizing that it would take very little to push Chiang Kai-shek over the edge, moving him from a state of simmering anger and galvanizing him into violent action. When it happened, that action was of such intensity and fury that the CPC would hardly believe it. Not in their wildest dreams had the Communists ever thought such a response was possible.

Even so, for a while Chiang still hesitated. Wang had always been regarded as the more indecisive of the two men but now Chiang was displaying a similar degree of hesitancy. There was one advantage to delaying: the longer Chiang remained inactive the more numerous and efficient his forces became as troops that had been left behind in his mad scramble to reach Shanghai began to trickle into the city.

The formal militarization of Chiang's China, as depicted by the cover of *Liangyou.*

Chiang's diary for this time records "sleepless nights" and hours of indecision. No matter what he thought of Communist philosophy or the ambitions of the CPC and its Soviet advisers, no matter how much he might deplore their duplicity, these were men who had marched with him and fought alongside him. Could he really take direct action against them?

In the final reckoning, however, there was too much at stake and sentiment could not be allowed to have any part to play. In his first decisive action of the affair Chiang now decided to order any army units known to have sympathy with the Communists and the workers out of the city. It was a sound decision, placing them where they could have no influence on what was about to happen. After that he sat back to consider his next move.

The picture was not pretty. Wherever you looked in China there seemed to be nothing but chaos and disruption. Strikes, riots, running gun battles—there seemed to be no end to the violence. And Chiang Kai-shek thought he knew where the troubles had started and where they would end: the Communist Party of China.

5. WHAT TO DO AND WHY TO DO IT

From the moment the first fires had erupted in the city of Nanking back in March, Chiang Kai-shek had always known that the Communists—either in the army or as independent members of the CPC—had been the driving force behind the Nanking Incident. If he had needed any further proof of their perfidy, the general strike that had so recently crippled Shanghai and many other parts of China was evidence enough. End the prevarication, he decided: it was time to act.

At this stage Chiang Kai-shek had already displayed his ruthless streak. He was not afraid of taking unilateral action but he was still not a dictator. He consulted with other leaders of the Kuomintang and ensured that he had their support—as far as possible—in whatever he was planning. There was never going to be total agreement and the finer points of the operation, however that operation eventually manifested itself, would be sure to bring disagreement. But no one in the KMT could ever say they were unaware that a reckoning was on the way.

NRA troops on the march. (Arthur Rothstein)

On 2 April the Central Control Committee of the KMT met and, under Chiang's direction, came up with a resolution to "cleanse the organization" of Communist influence. For the moment the resolution remained secret but as with all cloak-and-dagger agreements it proved impossible to keep the decision totally under wraps. Rumours quickly began to spread across the city: there was to be a coup, Chiang was going to kill everyone, the Nationalists were about to shell the city—and the tension increased: "As far as his eye could reach there was not a shop remaining open. He must leave as quickly as possible; he got out, called a rickshaw. The coolie did not answer him: he was running at top speed for shelter ... Two sirens, in unison, an octave higher, the cry of the one that had just died down, as if some enormous creature, enveloped in this silence, were thus announcing its coming. The entire city was on guard."[*]

Five days later KMT leaders met to discuss the recent activities of the Communists. Chiang obviously took the lead but, after intense discussion, the vast majority of those present seemed happy to share his views. Concern about Communist activities in all of the various territories or parts of China was widespread and the general feeling was that enough was enough: there needed to be a purge.

Two days after that, on 9 April, Chiang declared martial law in Shanghai. He reinforced the declaration with patrols of soldiers, effectively neutering the strength of the unions and bringing the general strike to a halt. At the same time the Central Control Committee of the KMT issued a proclamation, 'The Party Protection and National Salvation'. Among other things the proclamation denounced the Wuhan National Government's policy of cooperation with the CPC.

Chiang Kai-shek had had links with the Shanghai underworld for many years. Now, in a deal brokered by the policeman-gangster Huang Jinrong, he and the Green Gang leader came to an agreement. Du Yue-sheng would send in his men to help Chiang and in return his organization would face no punishment. There would be no retribution, no matter what damage was done. Neither Chiang nor Du stipulated what such damage might be but everyone knew it would be considerable.

There was also an agreement that once the Communists and trade unionists had been dealt with, Du would be given a monopoly on narcotic sales and dealings in the city. That was a lucrative dispensation and not one that 'Big-Eared Du' was ever going to turn down.

So much for the build-up to the massacre; Chiang had laid his plans and was finally ready to act. On the morning of 12 April he struck.

---

[*] Malraux

Execution!

Unleashed at last, 2,000 members of the Green Gang, the worst thugs that the mobster Du Yue-sheng could find, went to work. Together with the soldiers of the 26th Army they cut a bloody swathe across the city of Shanghai. It was a ruthless and bloodthirsty culling of Chiang's opponents and potential opponents with little or no mercy shown to anyone likely to obstruct his plans for the future.

The Communists had been expecting an attack of some sort but, apart from the few militia units commanded by Zhou Enlai, they had made virtually no defensive preparations, seeming to think that words were their best means of protection. Such naïveté was meat and drink to men like Chiang and, of course, to the Green Gang. As with any massive operation such as this, an operation involving hundreds or even thousands of men, once it had begun it proved almost impossible to stop: once the Green Gang was unleashed its members became a law unto themselves, not dissimilar to the military where once the army units went into action control over their behaviour came down to the local commanders.

That is not to say that Chiang was unhappy with what went on. On the contrary, he was more than pleased with what he saw as the destruction of the Communists as a militant force within China. But he undoubtedly distanced himself from the actual killings. From the moment the 4 a.m. bugle call announced the start of the operration, most of the murder and mayhem in the city quickly passed beyond his direct control. Chiang Kai-shek stood apart from the killings of the Shanghai Massacre. It was his idea, his plan, but the events within the microcosm were, by necessity, divorced from his personal command. Any images of him striding

Across the city executions, by sword and pistol, took place.

the streets, sword and pistol in hand, belong to the realms of fantasy. Distance, of course, allowed the Green Gang to loot what they liked; that had always been part of the agreement between Du and Chiang. But it also opened up the KMT to criticism from the wider world. No matter, Chiang Kai-shek could endure that as long as the operation achieved all that he wanted.

Chiang knew when he launched the first killings that it would not stop there. In order to eradicate the Communist influence those initial murders would have to be followed up by many more. They would have to be followed up by what became known as the White Terror.

On 11 April, the day before the massacre, secret messages were sent to all provinces under Nationalist control, ordering the purging of Communists from the KMT. When they saw the words "purging from the KMT" most Nationalists read that simply to mean they should exterminate the Communists wherever they could be found. If that involved violence, many thought, then so much the better.

The Shanghai Massacre unleashed an orgy of fury against the Communists, a killing spree that settled like a plague of locusts across the land. Perhaps as many as 12,000 died in Shanghai alone, 300,000 in other parts of China in the months following 12 April. Those are figures that should never be taken lightly. But it was what the massacre spelled for the future of the country—and arguably for the world—that really make it such a significant event.

Big-Eared Du—Bound for a Life of Crime

If ever there was a man whose background and upbringing destined him for a life of crime it was Du Yue-sheng, the infamous Big-Eared Du as he was universally known. Leader of the Green Gang, he was one of the most important figures in Shanghai during the first half of the 20th century and he achieved this by excelling at his chosen profession of crime.

Du was born in 1888 in the remote town of Gaoqiao. Just a year later, however, the family moved to the thriving metropolis of Shanghai, like thousands of other rural Chinese looking for a better life. Then things quickly began to go wrong for Du.

By the time he was nine years old he had lost all of his immediate and closest family. His mother died giving birth to another child and his father soon followed her to the grave. The father had remarried but once her husband was dead, Du's stepmother simply vanished. She was never seen again. Du's sister was sold into slavery and that left the nine-year-old orphan alone and vulnerable.

With no other recourse, Du left Shanghai and returned to Gaoqiao where he lived with his aged grandmother. The quiet little town was certainly not what Du Yue-sheng was used to and the restrictions imposed on him by his grandmother were unwelcome and ineffective. What Du needed was a strong paternal figure but, quite simply, this he never had. Unable to cope with the slow pace of life in Gaoqiao, Du soon left the place of his birth and went back to Shanghai. In 1902 he found work on a fruit stall in the French Concession but was soon fired for theft. Inevitably he graduated to the seamier side of life and by the time he was sixteen he was working as a bodyguard in a brothel. That same year he became a member of the Green Gang.

Du became friendly with Huang Jinrong, a corrupt police chief, and rose steadily through the ranks of the gang. When he bailed Huang out of prison—where he had been sent for publicly beating the son of a local warlord—the former policeman decided that enough was enough and handed over all his contacts and his position at the top of the criminal tree to Du. Big-Eared Du was on his way to becoming the grandmaster of crime in Shanghai.

NRA artillery attacking Communist forces, early 1930s. (CIA)

The Chinese Civil War that continued in all its bloody intensity until 1950 really began with the massacre. Everything that followed—Chiang's eventual defeat, the implementation of Mao Zedong's equally bloody regime, the Chinese involvement in the Korean War, the stand-off and the threats between China and the US—it all began with the Shanghai Massacre of 1927. Viewed objectively, it can be argued that Chiang had inleashed his wave of terror a little too early. In April 1927 there were still large areas of the country, particularly to the north of the Yangtze, that were not yet under KMT control. Unfortunately for Chiang it was something of a Catch-22 situation.

He could not finish off the warlords of the north until he had eliminated the threat of the Communists in his rear. And he could not deal, effectively and totally, with the Communists until he had destroyed the warlords and brought all of China under his control. It was the ultimate dilemma, one that would eventually destroy his fragile grip on the country.

The Northern Expedition had stopped more or less along the line of the Yangtze, thus allowing the survivors of the massacre, people like Mao Zedong and Zhou Enlai, to escape to the rural areas of the north, areas beyond influence of the Kuomintang.

And there, forced underground, running for their lives and hiding in the hills and forests, Mao, Zhou and the others were able to regroup and lay their plans for the future.

So why did the massacre take place? What did Chiang hope to achieve? Complex questions that deserve considerable thought.

To begin with Chiang had become increasingly disenchanted with the Communists he encountered and had tried to work with in China. In 1927 the CPC was still a relatively young organization. From small beginnings when Sun Yat-sen allowed their admission to the KMT to the formation of the Communist Party of China in 1921 it had been a remarkable journey. Young it may have been but as Moscow had hoped and Chiang had feared, the Communists had grown stronger and more powerful by the day. It was, perhaps, symptomatic of the times, Communist activity and influence mushrooming out of all proportion across the world.

The 1920s and 30s was an age of extremes in politics, the catalyst of the First World War seeming to have pushed people out of the age-old idea of acceptance and acquiescence. The traditional values of the past, with rulers and ruled, everyone knowing their place, were no longer good enough. One thing was certain, the words from the Victorian hymn 'All Things Bright and Beautiful' no longer applied: *The rich man in his castle / The poor man at his gate / God made them high and lowly / And ordered their estate.*

Above all, people now wanted a say in the way things were done. They demanded involvement in the way their countries were governed and led. It was no longer good enough to leave all of that to the traditional ruling classes. The upper or ruling classes had failed, and failed dismally.

From Russia to Germany, from Italy to Turkey, political parties on the far left and the far right were now making their presence felt. As with any change the process was often painful. You had only to look at the chaos of the German streets where the Fascist stormtroopers of Adolf Hitler were clashing, daily, with the Communists and the Social Democrats to see the truth of that. China was no different, having so recently emerged from imperial dictatorship, her people wanting at least some of the equality that the Communists promised.

To a right-wing politician and general like Chiang Kai-shek the Communist ideals were anathema. He had never been close to Borodin and the other Russian advisers but he had been willing to work with them, up to a point—to use them would be the cynical but probably more accurate assessment or viewpoint. And when he looked at the chaos their machinations had caused—and would no doubt continue to cause—Chiang was not just angry, he was frightened. Once he acknowledged that, his dislike moved from a political and ideological stance to a very personal position.

Over the previous few months Chiang had increasingly become a target for the CPC. It was understandable, considering his politics and his recent actions against

Wang Jingwei, but like many significant warlords of both past and present Chiang Kai-shek had a firm belief in his own publicity. It was the cult of the personality turned on its head and, at the most basic level, he had had enough criticism from people he neither liked nor admired. The Chinese Communists had angered Chiang by advocating—and, where possible, implementing—land reforms across China. Such practices upset the delicate balance of Chinese society and gave the people false hope. There would be changes, Chiang insisted, of course there would—but not yet. The blatantly undemocratic moving of the capital from Beijing to Wuhan—short lived as it was—gave him yet another reason to actively abhor the Communists.

He had tried to reach a compromise—so, too, had Mikhail Borodin. In December 1926 the two men had met at Kuling, high in the mountains. The meeting ended in failure, just like Chiang's trip to Wuhan the following month when he and the Communist leaders finished their meeting by engaging in a fierce shouting match. Clearly, Chiang and the Communists had reached an impasse.

But it was not just the Communists of the CPC that were causing Chiang sleepless nights. More than anything he feared the power and the influence of the Soviet Union. In 1923 when Sun Yat-sen first agreed to accept aid from Moscow, Chiang was sent to Russia on a three-month mission on behalf of the Kuomintang. He studied the Soviet military, the Soviet state apparatus and the Soviet Communist Party. He visited farms and factories, moved from one city to the next. And what he saw failed to impress him. He later described the city of Petrograd as "desolate" and found the people unhappy and depressed. Contrary to Soviet propaganda there were, he noted in his diary, "acute problems with the equitable distribution of benefits." In particular he was not impressed by what he considered an excessive centralization of power and control—an interesting comment that seemed to have little or no connection to his own political stance and later actions. Chiang's opinions might well have been influenced by the fact that, during this visit, he failed to attract Soviet support for an attack against the northern warlords of China—an idea that culminated, without Russian help, in the Northern Expedition of 1926/27. Nevertheless, he returned from Russia after a few months calling the Soviets "conceited and autocratic".

Chiang warned his colleagues in the KMT not to trust the Russians. They were insidious and cunning. More importantly, when he looked at the Communist Party of China he could not help but see them as agents of the Soviet Union. The activities of the adviser Mikhail Borodin did nothing to alleviate his fears.

As a Nationalist, Chiang Kai-shek was unequivocally pro-Chinese. He was afraid that the Soviet Union would extend its power into his homeland and there is little doubt that his decision to cull the Communists in China was a case of him getting the first punch in.

He still needed support in the KMT if he was going to put his ideas into operation, but it was not just in the KMT: he needed funding if he was going to launch the long-delayed Northern Expedition, eliminate the northern warlords and expel the hated foreigners, something that had been the dream of Sun Yat-sen, the so-called father of the nation.

The elite of Chinese society, the landlords and the industrialists, also feared the Communist threat. As capitalists and financiers their position was understandable. Whatever he thought of them on a personal level, Chiang could not afford to ignore this powerful lobby and he acted knowing that these people would be more than happy with what was being done.

There was also the small matter of self-preservation. At one stage he learned that the CPC, along with its Soviet advisers, were planning to take control of Shanghai, to lever its economy and its foreign affairs out of the hands of the Nationalists. The general strike, Chiang feared, was just the start, the thin edge of the wedge. He knew that if the Communists managed to take control of Shanghai it would spell the end of him as a military and political force in the country.

Memorial to Chiang Kai-shek in Taiwan.

Death was a constant factor in 1920s' China, just as it had been for centuries. Chiang had seen many of his friends and colleagues fall to the assassin's bullet and, like so many other leaders of the time, he was painfully aware that there were people out there who, for a price or a principle, would be only too willing to eliminate him.

There can be no doubt that some of the political killings over the years had been carried out at Chiang's behest, some even by his own hands. He was under no illusion: he was an obvious target and in a country that dealt easily in surreptitious assassination there was little he or his guards could do when faced by a determined foe, someone who was willing to lay down his life in order to achieve his goal: "He repeated to himself that this man must die—stupidly, for he knew that he would kill him. Whether he was caught or not, executed or not, did not matter."*

Faced by such fervour and determination, Chiang Kai-shek had just one answer: he would have to act first. And, of course, he did, on 12 April 1927. It is impossible to uncover all of Chiang's motives. His diaries speak, in the main, of his detestation of the Communists and that, obviously, has to be the driving force. It is the brutality that was used that shocks our, possibly, more refined senses. But this was a brutal time and in China in the 1920s there was no room for leaders who were not prepared to take the hard line. Chiang was certainly willing and able to do that.

He was always single-minded as the virtual abandonment of his son to the tender mercies of Stalin and his regime clearly shows. Driven and committed to the success of what he saw as his mission, this was no time for niceties. He would do whatever was needed, even if that meant personal discomfort or pain.

Whatever his motives, the Shanghai Massacre and the White Terror that followed it caused an irrevocable split between the KMT and the left-wing idealists of the CPC. In the months that followed, the CPC was removed from government in Wuhan and, both internally and internationally, Nanking became recognized as China's legitimate seat of government.

Once he was free of the Communist threat, Chiang felt able to return to his battle against the northern warlords without fear of being stabbed in the back by the CPC. The Communists, of course, had a very different agenda from him. For them the revolution, the Communist revolution which would mirror Russia's, was all that mattered.

Unshackled and freed of the Communist problem Chiang's Northern Expedition was a campaign that went on for some time. It took effort and it took vast amounts of money but it was ultimately successful.

---

* Malraux

Revolutionary soldiers on the Shanghai Daodai's yamen. (Francis Stafford)

Wang Jingwei, when he returned from exile, felt he had no alternative but to remain within the Kuomintang. He had never been a Communist or, for that matter, a great friend of Chiang Kai-shek's. Despite many bitter arguments with Chiang, however, he was able to work with the man he had hoped to replace at the head of the KMT and, ultimately, as the leader of the Chinese People's Republic.

It is doubtful that Chiang ever regretted his decision to unleash the Green Gang in April 1927. He was a man who was always willing to back up his ideas with action and he never once admitted that he had made a poor decision. The Shanghai Massacre happened, now it was over and done with—time to move on to the next problem.

6. AFTER EFFECTS

The effects of the Shanghai Massacre were many. Perhaps the most obvious was that, by his ruthlessness or by his guile—depending on your stance—Chiang Kai-shek had elevated himself to the position of leader of the Republic of China. In the words of Tien-wei Wu, the massacre had "established Chiang Kai-shek's hegemony in China for the next two decades and inflicted a ten-year defeat upon the Chinese communists."[*]

Chiang had effectively, on the surface at least, eliminated most of his opposition. That left him at the top of the tree, without any immediate challengers. On 10 October 1928 he was made Director of the State Council, the equivalent of president. For the next few years, the western media, happy to glorify him and be a part of creating a legend, invariably wrote about him as 'the Generalissimo'.

Internationally, in the 1920s and 1930s there was always a degree of affection toward Chiang, particularly in the US. His picture regularly appeared on the front pages of newspapers and magazines—on no fewer than eight occasions during the Second World War alone—usually astride a war horse and looking suitably martial. But even then, in that "low, dishonest decade" before the Second World War, American abhorrence of Communism was beginning to grow. In what had by then developed into the most significant capitalist country in the world the very thought of left-wing political parties had become a 'dirty idea'.

Any American care and concern for Chiang were really little more than an offshoot of the country's hatred of Mao and his Communists. All affection for the Generalissimo was invariably going to be a short-term love affair and, like the wind, liable to change direction at any time. As an example, following Chiang's failure to destroy the Communist forces of Mao Zedong he was often criticized as being a poor general, critics conveniently forgetting that he often had to fight three enemies at the same time—the Communists, the Japanese and the northern warlords.

In hindsight it is clear that, in the wake of the Shanghai Massacre and the White Terror, Chiang Kai-shek and the KMT missed their opportunity to totally eradicate the Chinese Communists. It was certainly not done deliberately but by failing to eliminate Mao and other CPC leaders, Chiang had left a rump of Communist influence in the country, a rump that was eventually to prove fatal for his dreams and his regime.

---

[*]   Tien-wei Wu

Initially, though, it appeared as if Chiang's purge had been totally successful. The killing soon spread to places like Kiangsu, Szechwan and Kwangtung. The governor of Kwangtung was particularly violent in persecution of the Communists, arresting over 2,000 of them and executing most of them in short order.

As the White Terror spread across the country, Mao Zedong and Zhou Enlai found their refuge where they could, the farther away from Chiang and his Nationalist forces the better. Most of them fled to the countryside of central and northern China. In particular they hid out in the hills of the Kiangsi province where, in 1930 they were tracked down. Between 1931 and 1934 they were surrounded and then attacked by Chiang's Nationalist forces. Somehow they survived the attacks and in 1934 managed to break out from what had increasingly seemed to be an ever-tightening noose. Led by Mao Zedong, the Communists then began what became known as The Long March, a journey of several thousand miles from the central plains of China to the rugged hills of the north west. The journey was harrowing with the fleeing men at the mercy of the elements and pursued relentlessly by their enemies.

The march was one of supreme courage and has been called one of history's greatest ever strategic retreats. During the March Mao Zedong was elected to be the leader of the Communist Party, a position or mandate that he was to hold for the rest of his life.

The retreating Communists were pursued by Chiang's armies and had to fight furiously all the way. Again, by some miracle, they managed to keep the KMT at bay, finally arriving, battered, bruised but defiant in the northern province of Shensi.

Here, in this mountain bastion, the remnants of the CPC managed to establish an impregnable base. Chiang continued to attack them, expending huge amounts of energy and men in the process. It was no use: Mao and his men survived it all.

Perhaps the failure of Chiang to finish off Mao's Communists was more a condemnation of the Nationalist tactics than it was of Communist strength and determination. From both a strategic and tactical viewpoint, allowing the Communists to escape the bottleneck in Kiangsi was a disaster. So, too was the Nationalist failure to eliminate Mao and his men as they ran for the hills. It is difficult to know how this could have been allowed to happen but certainly, in hindsight, Chiang's army was later to betray more than a little corruption and poor organization.

Failure to destroy Mao Zedong was only the start; there was worse to come. Obsessed by his internal enemies, Chiang Kai-shek had ignored the presence of a foreign power that was arguably just as dangerous, just as deadly, as Mao and his Communists: the dynamic and ambitious Japanese Empire. In 1931 the Japanese occupied Manchuria, one of the richest and most economically viable parts of the Chinese Empire. Condemned by the League of Nations and by world opinion, the Japanese invasion was to prove just how toothless international peace agencies

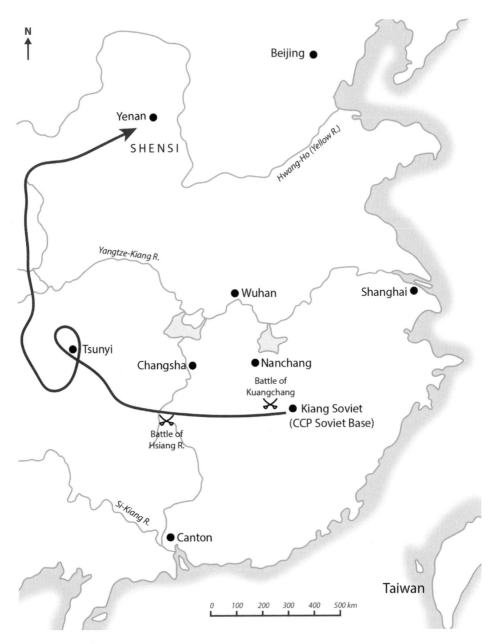

The Long March.

were in the face of determined and ruthless aggression. It was a lesson well learned by men like Mussolini and Hitler. The Japanese simply ignored all criticism and drew the Chinese Nationalists into a long campaign that would serve only to further weaken Chiang's forces and his position.

It was only five years later when faced by further Japanese aggression that Chiang realized he had to do more. Even then he was reluctant but despite all his principles he found himself forced into an alliance with the Communists. His hatred of the CPC continued to blind his judgement until his own troops and supporters managed to convince him otherwise.

It had been a difficult time and at one stage Chiang was even kidnapped by his senior officers who were desperate to forge a mutually beneficial alliance with Mao against the Japanese. He initially managed to escape the kidnapping and fled by climbing through a window, leaving behind his uniform, his false teeth and his dignity. Injured and cold, Chiang was soon forced to give himself up to his own officers and make the unpalatable decision to ally himself with Mao in the Second Sino-Japanese War (in reality part of the Second World War). It was a pragmatic move, not something that sat easily with Chiang, and he did it solely in order to keep the Japanese at bay. Despite being appointed Chief of Staff for the China Theatre (1942–45), Chiang could find little solace or enjoyment in the role.

After the defeat of Japan in 1945 the alliance was ended and the battle lines of the civil war were immediately redrawn. With barely a pause for breath, the internal conflict between Chiang and Mao began once again.

The final years of Chiang's regime were marred by infighting and a gradual erosion of his position. Bit by bit, yard by yard and city by city, Chiang was forced back. When Communist forces occupied Canton in October 1949 Chiang relocated his government to Chungking and on 10 December this last KMT stronghold in mainland China came under siege. The result was inevitable and when the time came it is reported that Chiang and his son Chiang Ching-kuo marched to their aircraft singing the national anthem.

It is difficult to take an objective look at what went on in China after the Shanghai Massacre. What is clear, however, is that the whole sequence of events—the gradual rise of the Communists and the demise of Chiang's Nationalists—was sparked off or begun by that one crucial morning in April 1927. It was not something that Chiang Kai-shek had ever imagined when he unleashed the Green Gang and his soldiers but what then happened to him and his forces was a clear and unequivocal result of the decision to kill the Chinese Communists.

Following the Shanghai Massacre, Chiang allowed Mikhail Borodin and the other Russian advisers to leave China. It was hardly a charitable decision but it was pragmatic. The last thing he needed was a dispute with the Soviet Union and he was not in the business of creating foreign martyrs.

Borodin was a major loss for the left wing of the Kuomintang. The Communists had already fled, gone underground, but is more than likely that the wily Russian had managed to keep in touch, with some of them at least. He had always been aware

This 1944 photograph originally bore the caption: 80,000,000 Chinese Communists who inhabit thousands of square miles of Northern China and are ruled, in spite of the Kuomintang, by Mao Tse-Tung and his Communist Armies. (NLFDR)

of the Chinese sensibilities, in particular their obsession with the concept of 'face'. To that end, in his negotiations with Sun Yat-sen, Wang Jingwei and others he had always made only suggestions, not demands.

Other Soviet advisers like N. V. Kuibyshev did not possess his skill or understanding of the Chinese character. Their intractability and stern "Russian Faces" did not endear them to the Chinese who always had something of a soft spot for Mikhail Borodin.

Borodin left China in 1929, travelling by train to Moscow. His time in the country had not been totally successful and he was leaving for what must have looked like an unsure future. His opinion of China was good, his feelings about the Chinese revolution more uncharitable: "The revolution extends to the Yangtze. If a diver were sent down to the bottom of this yellow stream he would rise again with an armful of shattered hopes."*

---

*   Mikhail Borodin, in Jonathan Spence *The Search for Modern China*

After Effects

The massacre and the ensuing purge set off something of a firestorm in Moscow. An emergency meeting of the Central Committee was held on 13 April, the day after the initial bloodletting in Shanghai, to discuss the failure of Soviet policy in China. Stalin had persuaded the Chinese Communists to side with Chiang and the purge undoubtedly presented him with a major setback. He was not yet as secure in his position as he later became and he now found himself facing a significant challenge to his leadership. It would require every ounce of his political muscle for him to survive. The challenge came, in particular, from his old adversary Leon Trotsky and a man he had, until relatively recently, considered an ally, Grigori Zinoviev.

Trotsky and his new ally Zinoviev were both conscious of the opportunity that had presented itself. The Shanghai massacre of Chinese communists and the virtual eclipse of the CPC had given them a wonderful chance to challenge Stalin for leadership of the party in Russia and, hopefully unseat him before he became too powerful. It was too good a chance to miss. Both of them considered Stalin something of a rogue elephant; they knew his character and knew also that if they failed to remove him now their positions would be untenable. Zinoviev had written a fifty-five-page document attacking Stalin's leadership and this was now distributed to the Politburo. For a while it looked as if their coup might had succeeded.

Unfortunately for Trotsky and Zinoviev, Stalin controlled too many votes in the Politburo and Central Committee and, as a consequence, favours were called in and the document was dismissed. The battle continued for a while but it was clear to everyone that there could only be one winner. On 12 November both Trotsky and Zinoviev were expelled from the party. Stalin had survived the challenge. Trotsky went into exile and both of the failed plotters were later killed on Stalin's orders.

The Shanghai Massacre was a pivotal moment in the Chinese Revolution, the vast upheaval that began with the removal of the last Qing emperor in 1912 and continued, with a brief respite during the Second World War, until the final victory of Mao Zedong in 1950. During those years Chiang Kai-shek continued his struggle against the warlords of the north and against the Communist forces that he despised. It was a difficult and dangerous task. He did manage to bring about the unification of China, nominally at least, "but he lost both the zeal for revolution and the trust of the masses which characterized his early successes. In retrospect, despite the effectiveness of his coup against the communists, it may have doomed his career as a great national leader of modern China".[*]

It is difficult to look at Chiang's period in power without thinking that it was a time marred by missed opportunities. Any revolution is bound to have casualties, as

---

[*]   Tien-wei Wu

Shanghai, the old and the new. (World Imaging)

Lenin said, "Any revolution without firing squads is a pointless exercise." But Chiang, from a position where he seemed to have had it made, fell disastrously from grace.

The American public and, almost by default, the whole world continued to think of Chiang as an heroic figure, struggling to bring China into the 20th century. In the later years, during and after the civil war, popular opinion considered him a bulwark against the growth of Communism in Asia. The sad but undoubtedly accurate assessment made by General David Barr, an experienced American officer who had spent some time fighting with Chiang's army was, for too long perhaps, ignored or disregarded by the public at large. In Chiang's army there was, Barr felt, "complete ineptness of military leaders and widespread corruption and dishonesty throughout the armed forces".*

It is an opinion that mars the generally held picture of Chiang Kai-shek as an upright, resolute and determined public figure. Small wonder, then, that in his last years Chiang Kai-shek became bitter and disillusioned by the attitude of the Americans he had thought of only as friends.

It is hard not to conclude that the Shanghai Massacre, which might have been something of a short-term solution, was the trigger that ultimately brought him down. It was to prove the greatest political mistake of his life.

---

* quoted in Chiang's obituary, *The New York Times*, 6 April 1975

7. FINISHING TOUCHES

Without wishing to overuse the old cliché of players leaving the stage, it is probably useful to look briefly at the post-1927 careers and lives of the main protagonists in this story. In one way or another they were all significant in forming the China that we know today and therefore some acknowledgement of their future lives is important.

Chiang Kai-shek died from acute renal failure, brought on by a heart attack and pneumonia, on 5 April 1975. He had spent the last twenty-five years of his life on the island of Taiwan where he had fled and set up his government, the Republic of China, after his defeat by Mao in 1950. It was an ignominious end for a man who had walked with kings and debated the issues of the day with politicians and leaders like Franklin Delano Roosevelt, 'Vinegar Joe' Stillwell and Winston Churchill.

Chiang was ruthless and single-minded. Whether it was the right move or the wrong one he knew what he had to do in 1927—and he also knew what he had to do in the years that followed. Arguably his single-mindedness and determination to defeat Mao Zedong and the CPC made him blind to all other threats. In the short term his political skills were excellent but he lacked the strategic vision to look into the far distance and respond to threats before they became too real, too alive. The long game was never Chiang's forte.

After his defeat and flight to Taiwan he never faltered in his determination to return to mainland China at some stage in the future. Even after his death that determination to return permeated the thinking of family and followers alike: "For three decades his body lay unburied in a casket in a low building by a lake outside Taipei. To have it interred in Taiwan would have been an admission that his dream of returning to the mainland in triumph had been defeated."* Indeed, this single-mindedness undoubtedly contributed to Chiang's faltering reputation in the years after his defeat. He had one ambition, one motive, and he remained a driven man, perhaps even more so in exile than he had been when he was in power.

His part in the February 26th Incident also played a part in the way the world looked at him. In 1947, while the civil war was still raging, there was a serious anti-government uprising in Taiwan. It was violently suppressed by Chiang's KMT and many demonstrators and protesters were killed. Some estimates put the death toll as nearer ten thousand. The massacre was followed by a purge, reminiscent of events in 1927. It was, arguably, the return of the White Terror. Chiang never acknowledged his part in

---

* Fenby

The role of women in Chinese society has changed immeasurably in the last century or so. Here a Shanghai woman selling brooms and baskets poses for the camera, c. 1872. (John L. Thompson / LoC).

A century and a half later, a model poses with a Shanghai skyscraper in the background. (Jakob Montrasio)

the February 26th Incident and he certainly never apologized for the actions of his troops—just like he had never apologized for the Shanghai Massacre and the White Terror. The February 26th killings did, however, reinforce the image of him as a ruthless military leader who would stop at nothing to retain power and influence.

On Taiwan he set up a one-party state and built up the army of the Republic of China ready for a return to the mainland or, if needed, as a force capable of defending his tiny island from attack by Mao. It cost money, a great deal of money, and he was untiring in his demands for cash from countries like the US. Not for nothing did the wits of the western world dub him 'General Cash-my-Cheque'. It was all light years away from his early days in power when he was feted by the west and afforded the epithet 'Generalissimo'.

Chiang's death marked the end of an era. He had been ever-present in China and in the imagination of people across the world. In keeping with his vision of a one-party state he was succeeded by his son Chiang Ching-kuo. As the power of the Chinese Communist state grew and expanded, as Mao became more of a perceived threat, Chiang's reputation underwent some sort of revival. It was, once again, more fear and dislike of Mao than respect for Chiang and the changes in people's perceptions reflect the bitterness of defeat for Chiang Kai-shek.

Chiang's arch-enemy Wang Jingwei was never happy with the situation in China after his defeat by Chiang and although he remained within the KMT he was like a fish out of water for many years. The relationship between the two men was never easy and Wang must have lived for the rest of his life with the fear of the assassin's knife in his belly or a strangler's noose around his neck. Then, in 1937, Japan invited him to form a collaborationist government based in Nanking. Wang accepted and, in the days of the uneasy peace between the Nationalists and the Communists, found a useful role to play, albeit in the pay of the invaders. He died in 1944 just before the end of the war. It was probably just as well: the vengeance of both Chiang and Mao would undoubtedly have reached out to gather him in.

After the massacre and coming of the White Terror, Mao Zedong and Zhou Enlai remained at large. Chiang never managed to capture or kill either of them and the two men were active in a number of uprisings against Chiang's Nationalist government, the first of them as early as October 1927. Both men were prominent during the Long March and in the creation of the Communist state in the north. Eventually, of course, they succeeded in displacing Chiang to form their own government in China.

Mao Zedong became infamous in the west due to his reforms, the Cultural Revolution in particular, and for his one-party, totalitarian regime. Communist it was not but the country and regime he created were certainly powerful. As the first Chairman of the People's Republic of China, he was as autocratic as Chiang Kai-shek and happily accepted the epithet Chairman Mao. He took it with him to the grave when he died on 9 September 1976.

Zhou Enlai became the first Premier of the People's Republic of China. A skilled diplomat, he also served as foreign minister for the new China until 1958. His skills and abilities helped him survive the purges that eliminated many other top Chinese officials during Mao's Cultural Revolution and he remained one of the main driving forces behind the state.

Zhou's particular claim to fame was that he was the man who engineered and orchestrated the visit of Richard Nixon to China in 1972, one of the first examples of a thaw in the icy relationship between China and the US. He died in January 1976, a few months before Mao.

General Bai Chongxi, the renowned 'Hewer of Communist Heads' during the Shanghai Massacre was an important member of the Revolutionary Army. A Muslim and of Hui ethnicity, he served as chief of staff during the Northern Expedition and later ruled the Guangxi Province as a virtually independent warlord with considerable political autonomy.

His relationship with Chiang Kai-shek was not always easy and there were times of considerable antagonism between the two. He was considered to be a fair ruler of Guangxi but by some error of security he permitted Mao and the remnants of the CPC to slip through his territory when they were making their Long March. Bai served as defence minister of Chiang's ROC but was unable to staunch the power and strength of the Communists. He fled to Taiwan along with Chiang and died there in December 1966.

The mobster Du Yue-sheng was an important element in the effectiveness of the Shanghai Massacre. 'Big-Eared Du'—so called because of his excessively large ears—began his criminal life in Shanghai as a gambler and opium enforcer. However, he always had visions of a life beyond the criminal fraternity and, as a lover of fine food, expensive clothes and beautiful women, the opportunity of friendship with a man like Chiang Kai-shek was too good a chance to miss. Du fled Shanghai for less dangerous parts of the world during the Second World War and his return to the city after the Japanese defeat was not as pleasant or as welcoming as he had hoped. The citizens of Shanghai felt that he had abandoned them and were not slow to show their displeasure. He settled in Hong Kong until he felt the time was right for a return to Shanghai but died in 1951 before he could make the move.

The Soviet adviser Michael Borodin, real name Mikhail Gruzenberg, retuned to Russia in 1929, accompanied by Soong Ching-ling, the widow of Sun Yat-sen. His welcome was better than he had ever thought possible, considering the relative failure of Soviet plans in China. Within a few weeks he had been made deputy people's commissioner for labour and then moved on to a career in journalism. Over the next few years Borodin became deputy director of TASS and, in 1932, editor-in-chief of the English-language paper *Moscow Daily News*. It was the high point of his career, a position where his people skills and fine judgements could be put to good use. He survived the German invasion of Russia during the Second World War but, eventually, Stalin's hand reached out for him. He was arrested in 1949 as part of the anti-Semitic purges of the time and died in Lefortovo Prison in 1952, reportedly after being tortured.

There were several other, perhaps more minor, characters who played a part in the dramatic events of early republican China. These were fascinating individuals who all had some role in the momentous events around the Shanghai Massacre and as such they continue to demand a footnote in history.

The diplomat Adolph Joffre, the man who effectively brokered the deal between Russia and China, persuading Lenin to give his support to the KMT, did not survive Sun Yat-sen by very long. A friend and supporter of Trotsky, by 1927 he had become gravely ill but Stalin refused him permission to leave Russia for treatment. On 12 November 1927, in the wake of Trotsky's expulsion from the Party, Joffre shot and killed himself.

The Dowager Empress Cixi (1835–1908) of the Qing dynasty. (*Two Years with the Empress Dowager* by Yu Derling)

The Dowager Empress Cixi effectively controlled the Chinese government for nearly fifty years as the power behind the throne of several of the last emperors. In a male-dominated environment she had to use all her wiles just to stay alive, let alone run the country. A firm supporter of the Boxers in their rebellion, she has invariably been displayed in films and books as a scheming despot. She died in 1908, leaving the two-year-old Puyi to succeed to the throne.

The Emperor Puyi, last Qing emperor of China, had ruled for just a handful of years—most of those while he was still an infant and with the country governed by a regent—before his forced abdication in 1912. He was restored, briefly, to the throne by the warlord Zhang Xuan but this second reign, from 1–12 July 1917, was both badly conceived and unsuccessful. The immediate furore that sprang up across the nation convinced both Puyi and Zhang that a monarch was the last thing the country needed and Puyi retired once more into obscurity. A strange character, controversial and different with every person who encountered him, Puyi was bad tempered, intolerant and downright rude. He could also be charming and helpful, if the mood took him. A sodomite, a sadist, a lover of beautiful women, selfish, generous to a fault, Puyi was all these things but then, that was possibly to be expected given his upbringing and his life style. After the Japanese invasion of Manchuria he became, at the behest of the Japanese, the nominal emperor of the Manchukuo state which he ruled under the name Datong. When Mao and his communists came to power Puyi was imprisoned by the Russians for ten years as a war criminal. During Mao's Cultural Revolution he was placed in protective custody, for his own safety, and died in Beijing on 17 October 1967.

The man who led the successful uprising against the Qing emperors, Huang Xing, remains something of a forgotten figure. At the time, however, he was one of the most renowned of all the revolutionaries and was second only to Sun Yat-sen in the KMT. He was wounded during one uprising in those turbulent years, shot in the hand, and, consequently, was always known by the epithet 'the eight-fingered general'. A statesman and soldier of note, Huang was the first commander of the ROC army and, like his compatriot Sun Yat-sen, spent time in exile before leading his forces to victory at the battle of Yangxia. Sadly, he did not live long enough to enjoy the fruits of victory, dying in Shanghai in October 1916, aged just forty-two.

Hu Hanmin was, for a time, one of the main leadership contenders after the death of Sun Yat-sen. Implicated in the murder of his rival Liao Zhongkai, he was imprisoned and dropped out of the leadership race. Strangely, charges against him were never pressed, something that leaves the distinct impression that the whole thing was something of a 'set-up job' to get him out of the way and leave Chiang and Wang free to fight it out. Before too long Hui was released from prison but by then Chiang Kai-shek and Wang Jingwei had pushed their claims and come further to the fore. Hui never again challenged for the leadership of the KMT. Hu supported Chiang in the Ninghan Split with Wang but their relationship was never easy. He served as minister of transportation in Chiang's government but died in May 1936.

Chen Duxiu was, along with Li Dazhao who was captured and executed during the White Terror, one of the founder members of the Communist Party of China. An author and philosopher, between 1921 and 1927 he was the first general secretary of the CPC. He was the man behind the Shanghai strike and, therefore, a prime target for Chiang Kai-shek but, somehow, he managed to survive the massacre and ally himself with Mao. In later years Cheng quarrelled with Mao Zedong and was expelled from the party. He spent fifteen years in prison before being given parole. One of the few Communist leaders to survive the turmoil of the 1930s, Chen died in May 1942.

Soong Mei-ling, the wife of Chiang, outlived him by many years. She had been invaluable to the Nationalist cause, even undertaking a speaking tour of America in 1942 in order to raise awareness and support for her husband's forces in the war against Japan. Working to the premise of what Paul Fussell has called 'my enemy's enemy is my friend', after the Japanese attack on Pearl Harbor Soong Mei-ling willingly, and in cooperation with her husband, became a pawn in America's public relations campaign: "China was seen as fighting democracy's battle and personified by the steadfast Generalissimo and his marvellously attractive, American-educated, unafraid wife. In their image Americans saw China strong in will and united in purpose."* She was also unafraid of infidelity, as witnessed by her 1942 affair with Wendell Wilkie, Roosevelt's envoy to China. Dynamic and intriguing to the last, Soong Mei-ling died in New York on 23 October 2003, at the grand old age of a hundred and five.

Chiang's son Chiang Ching-kio enjoyed a turbulent relationship with his father. Studying in Moscow—under the Russian name of Nikolai Vladimirovich Elizarov— he was appalled at his father's actions in the Shanghai Massacre. Or was he? Many believe that his critical response to Chiang's actions was false. It was, they feel, a letter dictated and directed by the Soviets rather than a genuine emotion. Certainly he was detained in Russia as a 'guest' for several years so it is, at least, possible. According to legend, Chiang Kai-shek refused to even consider exchanging him for Russian prisoners, believing that the good of the country was more important than saving his own son. It would be in keeping for the man who refused to help his son

---

*   Barbara Tuchman, *Stillwell and the American Experience in China*

As Dr Sun Yat-sen's secretary and assistant, Madam Soong Ching-ling took painstaking care of his correspondence, newspaper clippings, translation and typing. This photograph taken in Shanghai in 1920 shows Madam Soong at work in the study room. (China Soong Ching Ling Foundation)

Shanghai's Hongkew Market as seen in 1910. (NYPL)

buy a new suitcase while studying in Moscow, believing he should learn to handle his finances better. At the direction of Stalin and the Soviets Chiang was sent to work in a heavy machinery plant in the Urals, a situation that lasted for ten years. Arguably, given Stalin's murderous regime, he was lucky to escape with his life. Stalin did finally agree to allow Chiang Ching-kio to return to his homeland in 1937. He brought with him his Belarusian wife and child and was reconciled with his father. After his father's defeat, Chiang Ching-kio accompanied him into exile on Taiwan. When the grand old man died Chiang succeeded him as president of the ROC and began to create a more open, though still authoritarian, regime on the island. He died in 1988.

China remains a distant and different country. It has had a murderous past but it has also spawned some of the most fascinating moments of the last hundred years. The old cliché—all power corrupts but absolute power corrupts absolutely—is a phrase that certainly runs throughout the turbulent times of 20th-century China. As such, the men and women who endured it all, those who survived and those who did not, were people of supreme courage and ambition. If it is for no other reason than that, they and their history deserves to be studied.

CONCLUSION

There are many fascinating individuals, people who walk through the narrative of 20th-century China as if they were characters in a novel. They are men and women who, by their actions, by their integrity or plain old-fashioned evil, grab the imagination and demand to be heard or understood.

From Sun Yat-sen, the 'Father of the Nation', the Russian adviser Mikhail Borodin to Mao Zedong and General Bai, the 'Hewer of Communist Heads', there are enough characters here to fill the pages of *War and Peace*. And yet one man rises above them all. He stands like a colossus above the map that is the ancient and historic nation of China—General Chiang Kai-shek, the Generalissimo, the man who for over twenty years held the future of his people in the palm of his hand. He was not perfect. He was flawed, wavering constantly between the need for action and the desire to do nothing. Ruthless, violent, unable to see the bigger picture, he was still a man who

Taipei, ROC, today a modern international city. (Luke Ma)

Upper-class Chinese women, c. 1880. (Lai Afong / Galerie Bassenge)

had set his star and followed it to the end. He believed in himself and in the right-eousness of his cause. He was brave, defiant in the face of danger and graced—or cursed—with a sense of honour and duty. Chiang Kai-shek was not above taking the law into his own hands. It is fairly easy to see him uttering the words of a later revolu-tionary, Fidel Castro—"Criticize me, condemn me, I don't care—history will absolve me." History's jury is still out on that.

He was self-serving, of course he was, but he was also altruistic, at least to a degree. He did what he did because he felt it was right for his country, because the alternative was too harrowing for real consideration. His judgement might have been flawed but at least with Chiang Kai-shek you knew what you were going to get. And in post-imperial China that was a rare commodity. Nobody can applaud or condone the killing of thousands of Chinese citizens, many of them quite innocent of any involvement in the struggle for power. We have to acknowledge that Chiang may have been wrong, very wrong, but we make that judgement from a distance and with a degree of objectivity that Chiang and the others could not possibly pos-sess. Chiang Kai-shek strides across the pages of history and, as a consequence,

Chinese women in costume dress, 2013. (Vancouver Public Library Historical Photographs)

across the pages of this book, like a real-life King Lear—flawed, clearly wrong in many of his judgements, but honest enough to adhere to his principles and see things through to the end.

THE YOUNG COMPANION
ANNUAL
1933-1934

友良
刊念紀年週八

Liangyou Annual 1933/34, 8th anniversary issue. There would be no place for the magazine in a future communist China.

The question has to be asked: If Chiang Kai-shek had been given the gift of foresight and been able to look ahead to the way events finally played out (not something for which he was particularly renowned) would he still have unleashed Big-Eared Du and the Green Gang on the morning of 12 April 1927? It is a fascinating question, an imponderable one. We cannot find an answer and it is doubtful if Chiang would have been able to either. The after effects of that one fatal day are still being felt, in China and across the world. That is certainly some albatross to hang around the neck of one man but the impression remains that Chiang Kai-shek would have been happy to take it on.

BIBLIOGRAPHY

Books

Chan, F. Gilbert & Etzold, Thomas H. (eds), *China in the 1920s*, New Viewpoints, London & New York, 1976

Duffy, M. N., *The Twentieth Century*, Blackwell, Oxford, 1968

Fenby, Jonathan, Generalissimo: Chiang Kai-shek and the China He Lost, The Free Press, London, 2005

Fussell, Paul, *Wartime*, Oxford University Press, Oxford, 1989

Hayes, Paul, *The Nineteenth Century, 1814 to 1880*, St. Martin's Press, New York, 1975

Malraux, André, *Man's Fate*, Penguin, London, 2009 (reprinted from 1933)

Morris, James, *Heaven's Command*, Penguin, London, 1975

Perry, Elizabeth, *Shanghai on Strike*, Stanford University Press, Stanford, 1993

Spence, Jonathan, *The Search for Modern China*, Norton, New York, 2013

Tuchman, Barbara, *Stillwell and the American Experience in China*, New York, 1971

Ward, Harriet, *World Powers in the Twentieth Century*, BBC / Heinemann, London, 1980

Diaries / Unpublished Works

Borodin, Michael, quoted in Jonathan Spence, *The Search for Modern China*. 2013

Chiang Kai-shek, diaries held in the Hoover Institute Archives, available online

Films (feature)

55 Days at Peking (1963)

The Last Emperor (1987)

The Sand Pebbles (1966)

The Soong Sisters (1997)

Periodicals

BBC World Histories, December 2017 / January 2018

Life, various

National Geographic History, January / February 2018

The New York Times, various but principally 6 April 1975

Time, various

Websites

https://en.wikipedia.org/wiki/Chiang_Kai_shek
https://en.wikipedia.org/wiki/Shanghai_massacre
https://en.wikipedia.org/wiki/Sun_Yat-sen
https://en.wikipedia.org/wiki/Wang_Jingwei
https://en.wikipedia.prg/wiki/Canton-Honh_Kong_strike
https://hwcahuffman.weebly.com/shanghai-massacre.html
https://wikivisually.com/wiki/Shanghai_massacre_of_1927
www.alphahistory.com/chineserevolution/shanghai-massacre
www.britannica.com/biography/Wang-Ching-wei
www.hoover.org/library-archives/collections/chiang-kei-shek-diaries
www.leftcom./org/en/articles/2009-0-21/china-1925-1927
www.socialistalternative.org/2017/04/12/china-90-years-chiang-kai-sheks-shanghai-massacre
www.spartacus-educational.com/Michael_Borodin.htm
www.totallyhistory.com/Chinese-civil-war
www.youtube.com/watch?v=GWPOTDNOO2E

The France town waterfront, or bund, Shanghai, 1901. (NYPL)

Index

Appendix: Contemporary *Liangyou* Covers

期一第　◀ 版出日五十月二年五十國民華中 ▶　冊一月每

THE YOUNG COMPANION

No. 1 February 15, 1926

上海北四川路良友印刷公司印行

Acknowledgements

Roger MacCallum, genius of the technology—don't know what I'd do without you, Rog, just keep doing it please.

My editor, Chris Cocks, who believed I could do this—even when I didn't

The staff of the Central Library in Cardiff.

Trudy, who was always there, at my shoulder, encouraging and keeping my nose to the proverbial grindstone. God bless you, sweetheart, wherever you are.

Phil Carradice is a poet, novelist and historian. He has written over fifty books, the most recent being *The Call-up: A Study of Peacetime Conscription in Britain* and *Napoleon in Defeat and Captivity*. He presents the BBC Wales history programme *The Past Master* and is a regular broadcaster on both TV and radio. A native of Pembroke Dock, he now lives in the Vale of Glamorgan but travels extensively in the course of his work. Educated at Cardiff University and at Cardiff College of Education, Phil is a former head teacher but now lives as a full-time writer and is regarded as one of Wales's best creative writing tutors. He writes extensively for several Pen & Sword military history series including 'Cold War 1945–1991' and 'History of Terror'.

ALSO BY PHIL CARRADICE

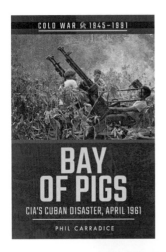

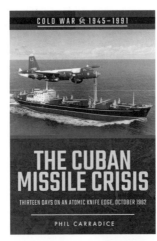

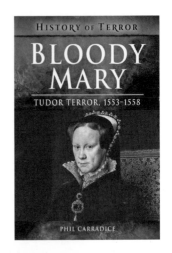

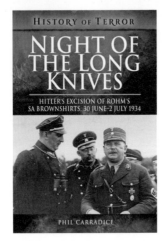

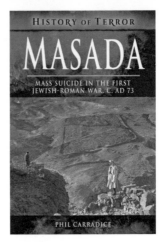